DATE DUE			

ODOR SENSATION
AND
MEMORY

ODOR SENSATION AND MEMORY

TRYGG ENGEN

New York
Westport, Connecticut
London

Copyright Acknowledgment

The author and publisher are grateful to the following for
allowing use of excerpts from:

Holley, André, *La Recherche*, 1989, vol. 20, pp. 172–173.

Library of Congress Cataloging-in-Publication Data

Engen, Trygg, 1926–
    Odor sensation and memory / Trygg Engen.
        p.   cm.
    Includes bibliographical references and index.
    ISBN 0–275–94111–6 (alk. paper)
    1. Smell. 2. Odors. 3. Smell disorders. 4. Psychophysics.
I. Title.
    [DNLM: 1. Memory. 2. Odors. 3. Psychophysics. 4. Smell. WV
301 E57o]
    QP458.E52   1991
    612.8′6 —dc20
    DNLM/DLC
for Library of Congress   91–21067

British Library Cataloguing in Publication Data is available.

Library of Congress Catalog Card Number: 91–21067
ISBN: 0–275–94111–6

First published in 1991

Praeger Publishers, One Madison Avenue, New York, NY 10010
An imprint of Greenwood Publishing Group, Inc.

Printed in the United States of America

∞™

The paper used in this book complies with the
Permanent Paper Standard issued by the National
Information Standards Organization (Z39.48–1984).

10 9 8 7 6 5 4 3 2 1

To Elizabeth Engen

Contents

Preface

When I started research on odor psychophysics most of my colleagues found it neither an interesting nor an important topic. One made the rather candid comment that one had either to be foolish or adventurous to take on a study of a sense for which there was no knowledge about the stimulus (as there presumably was for the more popular senses studied in experimental psychology). Research on the sense of smell has for the most part remained in the tradition of sensory physiology and psychophysics, searching for the stimulus and the receptor and how they interact. The assumption has been that solving this problem will make it possible to explain all of odor perception.

Assuming that odors are like colors, the standard approach to the stimulus problem has been to classify odors on the basis of how people label them verbally. Presumably, chemicals with similar stimulus properties activate certain receptors that, in turn, give rise to similar odor sensations. Odor classification has been attempted with many different methods but it has contributed nothing to the understanding of the sense of smell. Unlike colors, odors are not encoded at the receptor level but higher up in the nervous system, where odor sensations become intimately integrated with other information.

The sense of smell has become a more respectable topic in psychology over the years but it still suffers from benign neglect. Interest in colors is of course thought by all to be natural, but interest in odors is still considered to be quaint. The study of cognition has become a central topic but it has not included odor perception as much as one might expect. There have been some good but unconvincing efforts to show that the same cognitive principles apply to odor memory as to memory in general, as cognitive psychologists define it. One reason is that, for the most part, odor perception functions without conscious awareness while monitoring the chemical environment. However, what is interesting about odor perception becomes evident when one compares different sense modalities, especially with regard to memory.

To return to the stimulus problem, one cannot predict the response to odor, verbal or behavioral, from knowing the chemical. No odor, for example, can be used for commercial advantage because by itself it will increase sales. Not even a perfume will sell itself. There are no universal odorous aphrodisiacs or other odors that control human mood and motivation. Psychological effects of odors depend on acquired associations, which result either from first-hand experiences with odors or from suggestions (e.g., advertisements associating a famous personality—from Cher to Monet—with a certain perfume). Odors are evocative and the sense of smell docile, a quick learner, and that is a central topic in this book.

This is not to say that the stimulus problem is unimportant. Without excitation of the olfactory receptors by chemicals there would be no odor sensation, and research on the nature of this transduction is of fundamental importance. In contrast to vision, in which a sensation can be considered independent of the situation, odor perception involves a more intimate relationship between the perceiver, the odor, and the event. A certain odor is not inherently meaningful; it is a multimodal perceptual event rather than an isolated sensory event experienced as part of a larger whole to which it subsequently becomes a special mnemonic.

In some respects the sense of smell is inferior and in some superior to other modalities. What makes this "gateway to the mind" distinct are its special functions. Two of the more salient ones are the following. First, the sense of smell is a system for monitoring the odorous environment. Second, it categorizes odors from experiences with them and learns to ignore some and to approach or avoid others. Responses to odors are like old habits, some good, some bad.

The traditional approach to the study of the sense of smell is so-called bottom-up and is based on the assumption that odor perception is largely under the control of a prewired innate stimulus mechanism to be understood physiologically. The popular saying that "the nose knows" illustrates this. In contrast, the present approach is mainly top-down and psychological. It describes odor perception—and especially odor memory—as a special system, a schema, for processing odors. I call this the odor sensorium.

The book is based on the most recent research on how humans respond to odors and use them in adapting to the physical and social environment. The presentation is intended to be readable and nontechnical. The reader need only have an interest in odors, because this book requires no special background in psychology and physiology. It should be very useful as a supplement to courses on perception because the usual textbook treatment hardly covers any of the present material. The book will be of interest to perfumers, food scientists, and the various disciplines concerned with odorous air pollution. Loss of the sense of smell is a serious handicap, and therefore the book will also be useful to those who are interested in olfaction for medical reasons.

Acknowledgments

My research on the human uses of odor sensations started with a paper on long-term odor memory written with my former colleague Bruce M. Ross. It was Harold Schlosberg, the chairman of the Brown Psychology Department at that time, who gave me a job which made it possible to pursue such non-fundable research as the psychology of odor. The main support since has been provided by Birgitta Berglund and Thomas Lindvall in Stockholm.

Some young people whose interest in this topic has been important to me more recently are Gesualdo Zucco in Padoa, Steven Nordin and Mats Olsson in Stockholm, Magdalena Gilmore in San Diego, and Johann Lehrner in Vienna.

The manuscript benefitted greatly from Stephen Mayer's editorial experience. The manuscript was assembled and formatted by Michelle Ross. Finally, my thanks to the publisher for its efficiency and to John T. Harney and Alda Trabucchi for their personal editorial attention.

1

The Human Uses of Olfaction

The sense of smell is important to human beings and has always been so. The attention it has received has been greater at some times in human history than at others, and the attributes of odors stressed have varied from one age to another. Allain Corbin's book *The Foul and the Fragrant* (1986) describes how the impact of the sense of smell increased with industrial and demographic developments in the eighteenth and nineteenth centuries in France. Odors associated with poor people, latrines, and cesspools were suspected of being miasmatic and thus were to be avoided, deodorized, and destroyed. However, not all body odors were considered harmful. People of different social classes presumably emitted different odors, according to their different moral and intellectual characteristics. The notions of "the smell of the poor" and "the smell of death" are current versions of this belief.

While those in the upper classes feared that the odor of members of the lower classes would cause disease, they believed that the odors of their own classes were pure and sometimes even romantic. There were perceived differences not only in body odors but in the use of the sense of smell as well. For the poor, the stimulation of odors was assumed to cause impulsive lust, in inverse relation to intelligence, but for the upper classes odor perception was thought to have a higher purpose. Gentle folk appreciated the significance of different odors, while the poor were merely controlled by them.

The French government decided that odors in society must be eliminated, and "privatization" of human waste and body odor became a matter of public policy. Deodorization has been a serious concern ever since in hospitals, schools, and workplaces.

Although the class distinction may have largely disappeared, a dual role for the sense of smell remains. Odor perception serves both as a prototypical sensor for self-preservation against potentially harmful substances in the atmosphere and as a hedonic agent for the enjoyment of fragrances. One of these two roles has predominated at different times and places. For example, the hedonic agent was popular at the turn of the century, when the so-called *Freikörperkultur* and nudism stressed the natural, animal-like, and aphrodisiac attributes of body odor (Kern 1974).

The hedonic function of the sense of smell is the theme of the novel *Perfume*, written by Patrick Suskind (1986). This science fiction story describes the concoction of a very special perfume by a monstrous human being who himself emits no body odors but has a superhuman sense of smell. His unparalleled achievement is the creation of the ultimate aphrodisiac, distilling the essential odorous elements from the bodies of beautiful virgin girls.

Following the common belief that some odors are inherently good and some bad and that both types can motivate behavior directly for approach or avoidance, *Perfume* suggests that certain body odors, like musk, are aphrodisiacs. And yet, contrary to what popular advertisements would have us believe, odors are pleasant because they have pleasant associations. As Paul Jellinek pointed out long ago in the classic book *The Practice of Modern Perfumery* (1954), "Unless it is consciously or unconsciously connected with a sexual association, body odour cannot be called fragrant." Likewise, there is no inherent connection between lemon odor and freshness. The pleasant and unpleasant qualities are not in the odors themselves but in the events or persons with which they are associated.

The thesis of this book—that odor preferences are learned and that they function because of the memory of associations—may seem farfetched in the case of some odors. Who could ever be neutral toward the smell of diesel fuel? And yet some people actually enjoy it. More and more evidence is accumulating of the plasticity of the sense of smell and especially of the effect of early learning. Babies do not mind their own soiled diapers or those of other babies. Our own body odors are neutral or even pleasant, but those of others come to denote dirt and disease. Anything toxic makes one sick and naturally becomes unpleasant. Anything good or neutral could go either way, depending on individual—often idiosyncratic—experiences with it, which remain in the memory for future use.

Modern civilization, with its hygiene, plumbing, and ventilation, has contributed to the decline of research about odor perception. It is now a common opinion that although the sense of smell plays a crucial role for animals—all animals portrayed on television programs seem to be endowed with an extraordinarily keen sense of smell—for humans it is not significant. Thus, a recent review of disorders of the senses of smell and taste states that "many animal forms depend heavily on olfaction for survival in a potentially hostile environment. The sensory function of smell is overshadowed in man by his other abilities for interaction with the environment. Therefore, man has regressed developmentally in his olfactory ability as compared with most other higher life forms" (Estrem and Renner 1987, p. 133). Even if this should be true, with the increase in environmental pollution both indoors and outdoors, the importance of the sense of smell to humans may actually be greater than ever. This book attempts to present a balanced view of the human uses of the sense of smell.

The sense of smell is a sensitive, impressionable faculty for assessing the chemical environment and for storing information.

The olfactory receptors have axons that terminate in the olfactory bulb and thus they have a more direct connection with the brain than do the receptors of any of the other senses. Located high up in the nostrils, they still are in direct contact with the environment. They are exposed to harmful pollution, and perhaps as a result they have evolved a unique capacity for regeneration. We have some six million of them in each nostril, enough to detect significant environmental odors. Having many more receptors (perhaps two billion), dogs are even more sensitive. However, as I have noted already, the idea that humans need the sense of smell less because they operate on a higher intellectual plane than animals is a superficial observation. Not being able to detect odors is a genuine handicap. Mechanical sensors such as smoke detectors are useful in getting the attention of a person who is asleep or preoccupied and are especially important for a person whose sense of smell is impaired, but they are no match for the sensitivity of the sense of smell. For versatility, olfaction is in a class by itself.

At the same time, human performance in detecting and identifying odors is less reliable than sight and hearing are in detecting and identifying objects. Mistaken perceptions and even hallucination of odor are probably more common than in these other modalities. It is as though the sense of smell were guided by a rule not to miss any conceivable environmental signal, to maximize the likelihood of hits, but that in turn means that the number of false alarms will be high. We often think we smell an odor when none is present, and we are also inclined to overreact and perceive an odor to be bad before there has been enough time to identify its source. Only familiar and identified odors are perceived as good odors. For example, the other day I thought I smelled gas in the kitchen. It was a cold spring morning, with the temperature indoors hovering around 65 degrees, making the gas furnace go on and off. I checked the basement and found everything near the furnace to be normal. On my way upstairs I discovered the source: The coffee maker near the basement door was still on, with hot coffee evaporating. Side by side, coffee and natural gas smell quite different, but with a wrong mental set one is easily misled by the nose.

Folklore has it that "the nose knows" and can identify thousands of odors, but this notion greatly overestimates its capability. People can recognize familiar odors but are usually able to describe them only in general terms. Typical descriptions of odors are that they smell like onion, lemon, perfume, or excrement, or "like that old book in the library." Often one may recognize an odor as familiar without being able to pin down its identity, leaving one in the condition of uncertainty that has been called the "tip-of-the-nose" state (Lawless and Engen 1977). The nose is useful not because of its ability to identify odors "verbally" but rather because of its sensitivity, vigilance, and persistence in monitoring an odor until the odor has passed inspection by higher mental processes—and because of its ability to recall an episode involving a significant experience with it.

Whenever I smell new-mown grass, an experience from a faraway place nearly sixty years ago automatically comes to mind, as though time had stood still. It was the first experience of a city boy on a farm in the haying season, walking through a field of clover behind a mowing machine pulled by a homemade tractor. Everybody has odor memories that stand out because of the vivid way in which they recapture the past, including the feeling of the remembered event. This fact has contributed to the common opinion that odor memory is better than other kinds of memory. I will attempt to show that odor memory is a special system with certain outstanding attributes but that it is not generally superior to memory in other sense modalities.

One reason odor memory is so vivid is that it always involves odors encountered in the environment here and now. It is in fact limited to recognition; we cannot recall odors at will in the absence of such stimulation, as we can recall visual or auditory images. Such voluntary recall of the past is likely to be a prominent definition of memory in any dictionary, but the sense of smell is not capable of it. I cannot retrieve the memory of the haying experience by first conjuring up the odor of new-mown hay. The character Ganin in Vladimir Nabokov's book *Mary* has a similar problem in trying to recapture a woman's "cheap, sweet perfume called 'Tagore'." The author remarks that "as we know, memory can restore to life everything except smells, although nothing revives the past so completely as a smell that was once associated with it" (1970).

Most people believe that they can indeed recall odors, but they will usually agree after further introspection that what comes to mind is some object associated with an odor, such as the visual image of a lemon rather than a lemony odor. These related images do not bring with them the sensation of odor, and therefore they entail a different mental state than that elicited by the actual odors. Odor perception is multimodal, involving other sensations, including taste and the relatively mild irritation from stimulation of the trigeminal nerve, which become so intimately related that they become confused. This is the reason that losing one's sense of smell is experienced as losing the ability to taste.

A long-term odor memory can be established with only one exposure. An episode is tagged in memory with whatever odor happens to be present. And then, like a bad habit, this odor connection is difficult to unlearn and forget. One reason for this may be the overlap between central olfactory pathways and the parts of the brain—in particular the hippocampus and amygdala—that organize and store information from all the senses and provide its emotional tinge. Another reason it is difficult to get rid of an odor association is that it is not under cognitive control. One is not necessarily conscious of the odor at the time the association is formed. Of course, some odors are conspicuous, but that is not required for the formation of memories. Odor associations can be formed automatically and without conscious awareness.

The smell of the new-mown hay was not in my conscious mind when I was walking in the field. The scenery, my craggy-faced grandfather on the tractor, the special sound, and the feeling of a crisp summer morning had my conscious attention. The odor was only in the background as an incidental part of the whole perceptual experience. Nevertheless, the odor serves to retrieve the memory of the experience automatically and unconsciously. The French novelist Marcel Proust (1928) puzzles about his reactions to the flavor of a petite madeleine dipped in tea: "Whence could it have come to me, this all-powerful joy? I was conscious that it was connected with the taste of tea and cake, but that it infinitely transcended those savours, could not, indeed, be of the same nature as theirs."

Failure to retrieve a certain item in memory is generally caused by other items getting in the way. Subsequent events involving the item get in the way when one is trying to recall the first experience or association with it. In responding to odors we have the opposite problem. Having first learned one association to an odor, it is difficult for us to replace the association with another one. Odor memory fits the saying about teaching an old dog new tricks. This is why, for example, it is difficult to get over aversions to food flavors.

This domination of the first association relates to the way in which odors are committed to memory. An odor is integrated into the mental representation of an experience; it has no identifiable attributes of its own but exists as an inherent part of a unitary, holistic perceptual event. That is why it is difficult to identify isolated odors out of context. What we see with our eyes can be analyzed into colors, sizes, and shapes which help us describe objects and remember them. However, since these attributes are shared with other objects, they are also a source of confusion. Was the car a light blue Honda or a gray Mazda? As I have noted, odors do not have their own names but are described as smelling like something else, such as lemon or manure; for taste, on the other hand, there are such identifying attributes as sweet and sour, and for visual perceptions there are colors and many other features.

The special role of odors is to retrieve significant events regardless of when they happened. And it should be stressed that this is all that odor sensations do. They do not cause anything. When we feel sick in the presence of an odor, it is not really because of the sensation itself but because of the odor's association with sickness. Stimulation of the olfactory receptors has no other *direct* biological effect than to elicit odor sensations. Such sensations are epiphenomenal. Automobile exhaust smells; it is also deadly, but not because it smells. There is no innate olfactory mechanism one can rely on for sorting toxic from nontoxic substances. All the nose knows is to suspect anything with an unfamiliar odor.

But it is a powerful misconception that odor causes illness and motivates sexual stimulation. Even when one knows that it was not the smell of bourbon that made one sick but rather an overindulgence in it, the odor remains aversive as though it had been the cause. And such odor memories persist. In the story "Mosquitoes," the Soviet author Boris Bedney describes this attribute of odor memory:

The aromatic smoke unexpectedly reminded Vosboynikov of the half-forgotten scent of incense; his mother had been religious and had taken him to church in his childhood. He thought how unfortunate it was that his memory could retain this ancient smell, this early rubbish, to the end of his days, while it could forget more recent and more important things. This subconscious contraband was like dirt tracked in from the outside; he'd always carry it with him even to communism itself, these old and unnecessary memories (1962, p. 60).

The sense of smell is very sensitive, learns quickly, and does not forget, but it is not very discriminating and it has no judgment about what is important to remember and what is best forgotten. These attributes, however, ensure that among the contraband and rubbish will be information critical for a person's physical and psychological well-being. The sense of smell is a special system for responding and adapting to the environment, and that is what this book is about.

2

Odor Detection and Discrimination

The sense of smell has two interrelated functions: odor detection and odor identification. The human nose is in constant use, because environmental odors must be monitored constantly. For each odor detected, a memory search is made to determine its identity. One may know an odor without being able to name it, so that the identification need not be verbal, but if there is no memory of an odor and the odor persists, it causes apprehensiveness.

Familiar odors, such as those in one's car, are hardly noticeable; only odors that are somehow unusual or unexpected get conscious attention. Because the sense of smell is used automatically and unconsciously, its value is underestimated. This attitude changes considerably when it is lost. Patients often describe a mishap at home, such as failing to detect an odorous hazard, as precipitating a visit to the clinic to have their sense of smell tested. How often odor information is utilized by the average person would be an interesting and probably impressive statistic.

The sense of smell is a paragon of a sensor. Although the term clearly originates in the study of sensation, sensors are usually mechanical devices like smoke and gas detectors. While such mechanical sensors are limited to one or a few substances each, by contrast the human sense of smell is virtually unlimited in the number of different odorous substances to which it is sensitive. It not only motivates avoidance behavior but also may initiate pleasure seeking, which of course is beyond the capability of mechanical sensors. Fragrances are important for the sensory pleasures of people, both in interpersonal relationships and in the perception of environmental effects. But olfaction is foremost a sensor used to detect potential hazards in food and in the environment. Because of the potential survival value of the information it provides, this function might be the single most important factor in the recent renewed interest of this modality. It is the topic of this chapter, which emphasizes the role of unpleasant odors, warning signals of potential danger, and odors one cannot identify. Olfaction is also, of course, affected by subtler, more pleasant odors with quite different psychological and physical effects, as workers in the fragrance industry would be quick to point out. The pleasures associated with odors, including those involving interpersonal relationships, will be covered extensively in later chapters.

An odor whose nature and source remain unknown will keep the perceiver aroused, and prolonged arousal is a key element in stress, especially in a situation over which the perceiver has no control (Lazarus 1966). A persistent odor therefore is one of the symptoms of the so-called "sick-building syndrome" (Berglund and Lindvall 1986). This condition of psychological stress is caused not only by unpleasant or disgusting stimuli but even by hedonically neutral odors of unknown origin. By definition, an odor cannot be perceived as pleasant unless it can be identified. It seems natural to expect odors to affect one's health, and this expectation will affect one's well-being. If one is already not feeling well, as in seasickness, odor will intensify the problem.

Odor per se does not motivate behavior; rather, the relationship between odor and behavior is context determined. Where an odor is smelled is an important factor. Even body odor and tobacco smoke, which figure prominently in studies of indoor air quality, are not universally disliked, although they are generally considered objectionable. Being with friends at a party where people are smoking is quite different from sitting next to a smoking stranger on an airplane.

AROUSAL

An illustration of strong arousal by an unidentified odor is the following incident reported in the press. In connection with a program to promote safety, a gas company mailed its customers a scratch-and-sniff card containing the warning odor ethylmercaptan, which is added to the odorless natural gas. The odor was microencapsulated on the emblem of the company, a blue gas flame, which, when scratched, would release molecules of ethylmercaptan. For some reason, the molecules were released accidentally when the envelopes were handled in the mail. Since the envelopes had not yet been opened, it was not known what they contained, and this uncertainty made people nervous. The result was a large number of calls to the gas company.

In a context where it is expected, most people have learned the meaning of ethylmercaptan and will respond to it accordingly. In unfamiliar situations, however, they experience anxiety. According to another report in the popular press (Horak 1979), a gas company in Indiana received calls one night from customers worried that they smelled gas around the house. There were so many calls that the company had to resort to playing a recorded message stating that the situation was not dangerous. A subsequent investigation revealed that too much ethylmercaptan had been added to the gas, with the result that the customers were able to smell it from pilot lights and outdoor vents. Ethylmercaptan is added to natural gas in the first place because human beings are so sensitive to its odor that they can detect it in concentrations measured in parts per billion, and even a minor addition of mercaptan makes a large perceptual difference. At the concentration used as warning signal of gas it is harmless;

moreover, there is no innate avoidance response to ethylmercaptan anyway. A distinctive perfume could serve the purpose just as well. A novel odor will intrude even on a preoccupied mind, and the first, reflexive response to it is defensive. Ability to arouse requires a distinctive odor and a system that responds quickly.

The sense of smell is quicker to respond than one might think, considering the complexity of the nasal channel through which odorous molecules must travel before reaching the receptors high up in the narrow olfactory cleft (De Vries and Stuiver 1961). The timing of the presentation of odor is not likely to be as precise as that of lights or sounds, because the nostrils serve also as filters modifying what is let through. However, the latency of response to an odor before one can identify it verbally is surprisingly brief. In one experiment (Wang 1982) there was good control of odor delivery by starting a clock just as a subject sniffed and by stopping it when he reported perceiving an odor. The odor on any one trial was familiar to the subject from prior trials; odors included common ones such as oil of cloves, Pinesol, and chocolate. Odorless blanks were also included to check for false starts. The simple reaction time to an average of ten such odors was found to be 130 milliseconds (with a standard deviation of 45 msec). Slightly faster reaction times to other odors such as gernaiol and butanol have been observed in other laboratories (de Wijk 1989). The reaction time tends to be faster for stronger odors. Because of the difficulty of performing such experiments, the results can be considered only approximate, but they indicate that responses to odors are roughly comparable to responses to sound and light (Woodworth and Schlosberg 1954). There is no compelling reason to think that sensing an odor is a slow process. What slows down the identification of odor sensations is relating them to other instances of stimulation and other mental events.

As with any other stimulus, the ability of odors to elicit a response from a person depends on his condition as affected by drugs, fatigue, and general state of consciousness. One question that is often raised is whether or not an odor can wake a sleeping person. A sleeping baby will respond to a novel odor, as to a moderately loud sound, with a mild startle, but she will not necessarily wake up (Engen 1988). She will move and change her breathing at first, but then, after a few experiences with this odor, the baby will ignore it and will sleep on, apparently undisturbed. Recent research with adults using brain activity measured with an electroencephalogram as an index of depth of sleep shows similar results for even the relatively light stage 2 sleep just beyond the stage of drowsiness. Waking up during this stage may be perceived as having been deep in thought rather than asleep. Arousal was observed in only 39 percent of trials with a variety of moderately strong odors, including acetone. By contrast, an 800-Hz tone at 80 dB, judged to be at the same level of perceptual intensity as the odor, aroused the same eight subjects in 100 percent of the trials (Etgen, Wyatt, and Carskadon 1989). Deeper sleep would, of course, make arousal even more difficult.

Although people state that they think odors wake them, the experimental data suggest otherwise. Odors apparently would not make good alarms, despite suggestions by some entrepreneurs that pleasant fragrances can be released as a wake-up signal in place of the standard rude buzzing sound. They may affect dreams, but they do not change the sleep state, at least not sufficiently to be relied on for such a purpose. The odor of smoke alone would not wake one up in a fire. That is one useful attribute of a mechanical smoke detector. Processing of odors seems to require wakefulness and the ability to concentrate attention on environmental events, and odors may not be capable on their own of activating the higher brain centers.

FAMILIARITY

Naturally, familiar odors are expected to be well remembered and easily identified; therefore this was one of the first factors we assessed in a study of odor memory (Engen and Ross 1973). In one experiment we first asked each subject whether a certain odor was familiar or not, whether he could identify it at least in

Table 2.1
Preference for Familiar versus Unfamiliar Odors

	Liked	Disliked
Familiar	67%	33%
Unfamiliar	17%	83%

some general way. The second question in this experiment was whether the subject liked or disliked the odor. The experiment involved a large and diverse sample of odors; about half of them were judged to be familiar and the other half unfamiliar by any one individual subject. As expected, there were large individual differences in the responses to both questions. To me, the odor of ether means anxiety because of its association with a childhood tonsillectomy. To my wife, it calls back pleasant memories of her father's veterinary practice. To both of us it is a familiar odor, but it will probably not be familiar to the next generation because of the development of new anesthetics.

Table 2.1 summarizes the results of our experiments. Of the identifiable or familiar odors, 67 percent were described as liked and only 33 percent as disliked, a ratio of two to one. By contrast, only 17 percent of unfamiliar odors were liked and 83 percent were disliked, a ratio of about five to one in the opposite direction. In other words, even in this safe test situation where the subjects had been told that no harmful odors would be presented, there was a strong tendency for unfamiliar odors to be viewed with disfavor. It is important to note that different individuals knew different odors, and what the experiment showed was the relationship between familiarity and preference. That is, these results are individual response-response correlations, not odor-response associations (such as ones that might result from ethylmercaptan being disliked and lemon liked).

Table 2.2 illustrates the kind of odors one might find in each of the four categories of Table 2.1. An interesting problem is posed by the category of unfamiliar and liked odors. One can easily find examples of each of the other three categories, but this one is an exception. In the "familiar-liked" category are all the

Table 2.2
Odors Illustrating Effect of Familiarity on Preference

	Liked	Disliked
Familiar	flowers	diesel
Unfamiliar	?	strange house

pleasant associations one has had with odors, including odors of foods, flowers, significant other people, and places—in short, all of one's good odor memories plus the culturally designated good smells. These will be discussed in separate chapters on odors of foods and perfume fragrances.

The "familiar-disliked" category contains all the odors generally considered unpleasant in a culture, such as diesel fuel, plus all of one's individual dislikes. Odors in unfamiliar places would be likely to be put in the "unfamiliar-disliked" category. As an unfamiliar odor becomes familiar, it obtains its hedonic classification. A strange house could be the setting for a happy occasion, which then, in retrospect, provides new meaning for the house's odor.

Unfamiliar odors—for example, the odor of a strange house in a foreign place—while not necessarily extremely unpleasant, are always viewed with suspicion. However, Table 2.1 shows that some odors judged to be unfamiliar were nevertheless liked. The category is not empty but contains a score of 17 percent. Follow-up questions suggested that the reason involves the specificity of the definition of the world *unfamiliar*. To some subjects this meant that they could not name an odor although they were fairly certain about the kind of odor it was and its general category, such as chemicals including paint thinner and diesel fuel. My hunch is that if one could get beyond this semantic problem, the results would show this category to be empty.

Of course, there are general, culturally based agreements about some odors, but individual differences are inevitable. It should be emphasized that the results shown in Table 2.1 reflect individual preferences. Attempts to find general classes of liked and disliked odors fail because they are based on the false assumption that the hedonic quality of the odor is in the stimulus and is determined by its chemical or physical attributes rather than in associations with individual experiences. Of course, stimulus attributes are important factors explaining why it is that some compounds have an odor—that is, activate the olfactory receptors—and others do not, but it is life experiences that determine their meaning for the individual.

The first whiff of an odor does not stimulate intellectual curiosity, as the first glimpse of a picture often does; rather, it is more likely to put one on the defensive with a negative attitude until the consequences are known. Novel odors are responded to individually and are stored with other sensory emotional input. In particular, the odor of a situation in which one got sick must not be forgotten. The special and perhaps unique role of the sense of smell is to reinstate the past experience with odors, whether involving nutrition, odors of other people, or pollution. Recognition of odors from past experiences is important for survival, and memory is therefore a central topic of this book. The odor is not the only clue, nor necessarily the outstanding attribute of the situation at the time the experience occurred, but it is the clue most likely not to be forgotten.

3

The Persistence of Odors

There is much folklore but there are few established facts about the use of the sense of smell by humans. One popular belief is that the sense of smell is so easily saturated when exposed to a certain odor that its ability to perceive that odor lasts for only a few minutes (Engen 1982). A dog with that kind of nose would not be able to hunt. Animals use their sense of smell constantly and would not survive if sensitivity to odors diminished that quickly. But humans also use their sense of smell all the time, and under normal circumstances it keeps functioning through exposure to many different odors.

The problem of adaptation to odor is frequently confounded with other processes. There are two different categories of effects, each involving a different neural system. One is a so-called bottom-up effect, by which stimulation decreases the ability of the olfactory receptors of the peripheral nervous system to respond. The other is a top-down effect, involving processing of an odor sensation from the peripheral olfactory receptors by higher centers in the brain. It is important to realize that both of these processes affect an odor experience at the same time.

This chapter first discusses the bottom-up effect, which is properly called adaptation. It denotes a decrease in sensitivity to an odor because of a change in the function of the receptors, and this decrement may spread to the perception of other odors through cross-adaptation. However, depending on the pair of odors, exposure to one odor may also increase the strength of the response to a second odor, a phenomenon called facilitation. When the odor stimulus is removed or avoided, recovery from adaptation occurs.

The top-down effects discussed in the second section of this chapter involve the ways in which odor sensations are processed centrally in the brain. The intensity and stability of odor stimulation are controlled by sniffing. One learns to ignore familiar odors, and attention becomes selective through habituation. Because of special emotional experiences with a certain odor, a person may become sensitized to it so that it persists as a continuous annoyance that cannot be ignored.

ODOR EXPOSURE AND ODOR SENSITIVITY

The air quality of a room is evaluated better by having humans judge how good or bad it smells than by analyzing it with chemical or mechanical devices (Fanger 1988; see also Chapter 5 of this book). However, prolonged exposure to odors may diminish the judges' sensitivity and limit their usefulness. The odor of a room becomes less noticeable the longer one remains in the room and may in time seem to disappear altogether. Although the nature of the interaction between olfactory receptors and odorous molecules is not understood, it is clear that the concentration of molecules can exceed the ability of the receptors to handle them. This state is variously described as adaptation, fatigue, or, occasionally, stimulus failure. It is a common phenomenon affecting all the senses, and yet there is a popular but unproven assumption that adaptation has a greater impact on odor perception than on any of the other senses. There are two parameters to adaptation of the receptors in the nose. The strength of an odor stimulus is one; the other is how long the receptors are exposed to the stimulus.

Strength of the Stimulus

The minimum concentration needed for detection of a perfume in a large room is about one drop. However, prior exposure—as experienced, for example, by a saleslady at a perfume counter—would make a person less sensitive to the perfume, so that a greater amount would be required for her to detect it. The stronger the prior exposure, the higher the threshold of sensitivity. The effect of adaptation on odors encountered in the environment increases with the strength of this prior exposure. In other words, the threshold is affected, but the perception of an odor in a room saturated with it would hardly be affected at all. The effective stimulus range from the smallest detectable concentration to the largest concentration becomes shorter. This in turn decreases the ability to perceive changes in odor stimulation: the more adapted, the poorer the ability to discriminate between odors.

Duration of Exposure

For any single odor, the longer the exposure, the less sensitive one is to it. A change in the reaction of the olfactory receptors to odorous molecules takes place. This results in a rapid, exponential decrement in sensitivity, but except for the weakest odors, sensitivity does not diminish to zero (e.g., Berglund, Berglund, and Lindvall, 1978). The presence of a certain concentration of odorous molecules on the olfactory epithelium changes the response of the receptors to a much lower but relatively stable level, from which there is only a relatively slow decrement over the next thirty minutes or more. Laboratory data are available only for shorter periods (see Berglund, Berglund, Engen, and Lindvall 1971), but they support such a projection. A stronger stimulus, such as the salty smell of an ocean beach, will remain effective much longer.

Figure 3.1
Effect on the Perceived Strength of a Weak or Strong Odor as a
Function of the Duration of Exposure to It

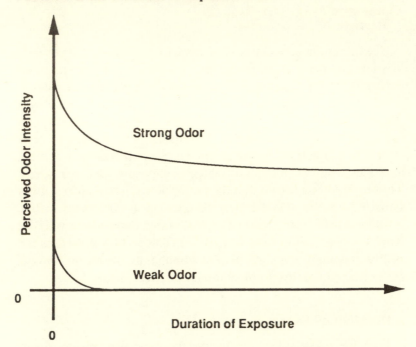

The effects of duration of odor exposure and concentration are illustrated in Figure 3.1, with the starting point of each curve, or the intercept, on the vertical axis. The different curves illustrate the effects of prior exposure to different odor concentrations. Temporal effects are shown as changes along the horizontal axis. The sense of smell operates as a signal-to-noise ratio system, in which the continuous presence of an odor acts like a masking factor causing an increase in the noise level, which in turn affects the apparent strength of the odor signal.

Table 3.1 shows evidence of the stability of odor sensitivity through continuous use of the sense of smell for about thirty minutes (Engen 1989, unpublished). In this conventional detection experiment, one subject was tested on seventy-one consecutive days with a weak concentration of n-butanol diluted in water.

Table 3.1
Percentage of Hits and False Alarms Based on 426 Judgments to a Weak Odor (N-Butanol) or a Blank (Water) for Each of Five Consecutive Blocks of Trials

Blocks of 5 Trials

	1	2	3	4	5
Hits	68	72	61	60	73
False Alarms	9	6	7	12	11

There was only a fifteen-second pause between each pair of thirty trials. The results are shown in terms of correct responses (hits) and errors describing plain water as the odor (false alarms). There is no evidence of decrement of performance or of adaptation. The results fluctuate, but they are nearly the same at the end of the session as at the beginning.

Cross-adaptation

Another part of the folklore about odor perception is that exposure to an odor will decrease sensitivity to other odors encountered subsequently. This so-called cross- or coadaptation is presumed to occur with odors that activate the same olfactory receptors. A practical consequence is believed to be that smokers, for example, will be less able to perceive and enjoy flavors of foods, in which odors play a dominant role. That may happen for certain combinations of odors, but such mutual fatigue is only one possibility.

All food flavors, flowers, perfumes, and pollutants contain many different chemicals, and the odors experienced in the real world are therefore always complex. Because of the demand for experimental control, most, but not all, laboratory experiments on odor adaptation have manipulated single odors. In an attempt to simulate real-life experiences, one experiment concerned with air pollution tested the effect of adaptation to a mixture of odorous pollutants on the perceived intensity of each of its components (Berglund and Engen, unpublished). Mixtures of dimethyl disulfide (DMDS) and hydrogen sulfide (H_2S) were presented with an olfactometer, which is an instrument for precisely measuring the concentration of odor. The adapting stimuli varied from a stimulus containing only DMDS through different mixtures of the two substances to a stimulus containing only H_2S. The target odor was either pure H_2S or pure DMDS.

Results showed that prior exposure to either pure substance had a greater effect on sensitivity to the substance itself than it did on sensitivity to the other substance. Consistent with that finding, the coadaptation effect was proportional to the amount of the target in a particular adapting mixture. In other words, the effect of adaptation tends to be specific to the odor to which one has been exposed. The sensitivity to an odor is reduced by prior exposure to it, but this effect does not spread to other odors. Therefore, appreciation of a perfume is not likely to be ruined by exposure to cigar smoke, for the two contain largely different chemicals.

Another coadaptation experiment reversed the order of administration of the mixture and the pure substance (Engen 1964). The odor of a mixture of amyl acetate ("banana") and heptanal ("castor oil") was now the target on which subjects were tested, following adaptive exposure to either of the single components. The results showed that prior exposure to banana made the mixture smell more like castor oil, and adaptation to castor oil brought out the banana smell of the mixture.

Such qualitative changes in perception are common experiences. A change in the perception of foods that contain mixtures of many components is not simply a change in strength but a change in flavor. Such a qualitative change is probably what results from giving up smoking. The perception of food is now different because increased sensitivity to certain odors has changed the pattern of stimulation and not because, as is popularly assumed, sensitivity to all odors is now greater.

Merely using the sense of smell will naturally cause some fatigue, regarding some odors more than others, and it will change but not abolish perception. Although weak odors may become imperceptible because of continuous exposure to them, stronger ones remain effective stimuli. A properly working olfactory system prevents functional anosmia by avoiding extreme stimulation and by controlling the amount of stimulation through sniffing. Overexposure does of course occur in certain environments, but the odors normally encountered, or those one lets oneself be exposed to, tend to be moderate. Listening to loud music affects sensitivity to sounds without upsetting normal auditory perception. Likewise, constant exposure to various odors affects sensitivity without interfering with the perception of significant odors.

Facilitation

Coadaptation effects are not symmetrical, even for odors with similar properties. For example, the perception of pentanol has a relatively strong effect on the perception of propanol, a closely related alcohol, but the perception of propanol has only a relatively weak effect on the perception of pentanol (Cain 1970). Moreover, for certain pairs of odors, the opposite of the attenuating effect of coadaptation has actually been observed. Thus, prior exposure to heptanol, for example, increases the perceptual strength of propanol (Corbit and Engen 1971; Berglund, Berglund, and Lindvall 1987; Laing and MacKay-Sim 1975).

The reason for this effect—which has been described as facilitation, synergism, or potentiation—is not known, but it is assumed to involve the peripheral olfactory mucosa, where an odor interacts with the receptors mucus. There are several possible mechanisms: An odor may alter the mucus around the olfactory receptors so that they are more accessible to the molecules of a subsequent odor (Mair, Bouffard, Engen, and Morton 1978); the two odors may involve the same receptors in some way so that their effects sum (Caprio, Dudek, and Robinson 1987); or the first odor may create a priming effect that enhances general chemical communication.

Recovery

The sense of smell is affected by exposure to odor but does, of course, recover from the fatigue associated with it. There are few data from laboratory research regarding the duration of the recovery, but it seems to be brief and to mirror that for the development of adaptation (Ekman, Berglund, Berglund, and Lindvall 1967). Workers who clean out storage tanks for heating oil during the late spring and summer become less sensitive to the odor of oil, but normal sensitivity to it returns during the winter. Smokers are less sensitive to pyridine, which is one of the sharp-smelling components of tobacco smoke (Ahlstrom and Engen 1987; Ahlstrom, Berglund, Berglund, Engen, and Lindvall 1987), but when they quit smoking they, too, report that their sense of smell is better.

The temporary decrease in odor sensitivity resulting from adaptation is analogous to a temporary threshold shift in hearing during recovery from exposure to a certain sound. However, perception of sound and odor differ in other respects. A noticeable and unexpected pleasure is felt when a noise to which one has become habituated suddenly stops. Such rapid change is not evident in the sense of smell, which is primarily an alarm system attending to the onset of stimulation but ignoring its cessation.

ODOR PROCESSING

The discussion so far has implied that environmental odors control the perceiver, but that is not the case. The active use of the sense of smell plays a part in regulating the number of odorous molecules reaching the olfactory cleft at the top of the nostrils, where the olfactory receptors are located. For that reason, odor stimulation in real life is highly variable even though the air may contain a constant concentration of odor. To begin with, in normal breathing it is estimated that only 5 to 10 percent of the air inhaled gets to the olfactory cleft. Most of it passes below, through the pharynx and past the epiglottis, and is channeled through the larynx to the lungs. Sniffing serves to vary the amount of air flowing through the nostrils. If an odor is weak, one can increase the stimulation by sniffing harder. Breathing through the mouth will reduce it. By simulating gagging one can shut off the access of odorous molecules through the pharynx between the mouth and the cleft. This control prevents overexposure and keeps the sense of smell working, even when it is used constantly as by perfumers and flavorists.

Odors activate the peripheral sensory receptors, but the response is modulated by an internal mechanism. We are not aware of it on our own breath, but garlic odor from another person is distinctly aversive. A completely reliable "deodorant" for this odor problem is to eat some garlic oneself. Having had garlic oneself means that it has passed an internal safety check. This is a bottom-up adaptive effect of bodily state on the sensory input. There is also an internal but top-down control from higher centers in the brain involving learning; that is, one learns to respond differently to odors because of personal experiences with them. Two principal mechanisms for this purpose, habituation and sensitization, both involve learned selective attention.

Habituation

Like adaptation, habituation entails a weakening of the response to an odor, but for a different reason. The effects on behavior and perception are similar, and it is not obvious from observing other people's reactions to odors—or even from introspecting about one's own experiences with them—which mechanism is operating. The two are typically confounded in discussions of odor sensitivity. While adaptation is caused by the fatigue of receptors, habituation is an adjustment to an odor based on an unconscious judgment that it is of no significance and can be ignored. Adaptation means that sensitivity to the odor is diminished and may be below threshold, but during habituation sensitivity is actually inhibited. Even though no overt responses are evident, sensations are still being registered.

Sleeping in a newly painted bedroom illustrates the difference. The paint job has been completed and the room put back in use just before bedtime. The smell of paint will persist after one has gone to bed and as long as one is awake. Although it will be weaker then because of exposure and adaptation, the paint odor is strong enough to be noticed when one wakes up in the middle of the night, and it will probably be there in the morning some eight hours later, but only if one directs one's attention to it.

Because both processes occur at the same time, it is not obvious how much of the diminution of the perceived odor strength is accounted for by habituation and how much by adaptation. However, experiments with the reactions of newborn infants demonstrate that the response to an odor can be inhibited while sensitivity to it remains largely unaffected (Engen and Lipsitt 1965). A change in respiration is one index showing that an infant smells an odor. To a naive infant with minimal environmental experience, any odor is novel. In one experiment, we repeatedly presented a chemically inert mixture of asafetida ("onion") and anise ("licorice"), with a pause of a minute between presentations to prevent adaptation. After some ten trials, the response had typically diminished or disappeared altogether. The odor was by then familiar and had been judged in some way to be inconsequential.

If instead this cessation of response were caused by receptor failure, the infants should not be able to sense either of the components after the response to their mixture had ceased. However, we found that the infants responded to both onions and licorice. The response was less vigorous either because of some adaptation or because the odors of the separate components were weaker than the mixture of two odors, but the infants could smell them. The chemical substances were the same, but the quality of the odors was now different and therefore stimulating. The strength of the posthabituation response to the components depended primarily on their novelty or the degree of dissimilarity from the odor quality of the mixture.

In other words, unless significant events are associated with an odor, attention to it will wane. However, the odor will still be registered and monitored centrally so that one can return one's attention to it if need be. Attention is selective. The odor of the freshly painted bedroom will not reach consciousness when one gets up in the morning and is busy with other things, but visual inspection of the previous day's work will override the inhabitory effect of habituation and will bring it back. Environmental and central nervous system factors interact.

Sensitization

Because of special experience with an odor, it may become extremely evocative. There are certain odors one cannot get out of one's mind. Like habituation, sensitization is an acquired response, but it has the opposite effect. Certain smells persist in consciousness and cause annoyance, as illustrated in a letter I received requesting information about what to do about such an odor.

The letter writer had an old aunt who lived alone in a single-family house in another state. The aunt died one hot and humid summer day, and her death was not discovered until three weeks later, when a neighbor became concerned. At that time one could smell the body outside the tightly closed house. Some of the cleaning people refused to return after removing the carpet on which the body had literally exploded. The niece, the only surviving relative, did not enter the house until it had been aired out for about twenty-four hours. The odor was still very strong, but as the representative of the estate she had to sort out memorabilia, important papers, and possessions accumulated over thirty-five years. It was a time-consuming job done in the stench. Months later she wrote, "I still at times smell the horrible odor, and it brings the unpleasant memories of that week cleaning out the home—is it something I may have to live with the rest of my life?" The answer was probably yes and I could only suggest to her one recourse: desensitization, which would require special behavioral modification therapy using a similar odor, a great obstacle in itself.

Sensitization is a special type of learning involving an association between stimuli which somehow must be unlearned and thus forgotten. It is as though sensitization had a straight pathway to the "learning center" of the brain and was more easily committed to memory. An odor is only one sensory element among several when such an odor association is established, but it becomes strengthened by what in the learning theory of Pavlovian conditioning is known as potentiation.* The odor does not even necessarily or typically stand out (as it did of course in the letter writer's case) but comes to do so in time, for two reasons. First, its strength derives from other sensory input. I have already noted that an odor is an epiphenomenal clue. In the case of food aversion, the strength of an odor is based on its association with the taste of something and the connection with the visceral system. Second, an odor sensation is more resistant to forgetting than other such cues, a topic that will be pursued in the following chapters.

Hypersensitivity can also be caused by illnesses such as Addison's disease and pituitary tumors. Such etiologies are beyond the present scope of this book, but the psychological effects of abnormal sensitivity are deleterious, no matter what the cause. The importance of the sense of smell is often only appreciated when it is impaired in some way, and hypersensitivity illustrates how stressful the mere experience of odor is when there is no control over it.

---

*Thanks to David Roe for suggesting this.

4

Monitoring Odors

Whenever we describe our environment in terms of comparatives, such as "it is getting lighter," "the smell of gas seems stronger," or "it's warmer," a memory of an earlier sensation is compared with the one experienced now. I use the term *sensory memory* to distinguish this kind of memory from the more familiar notion of long-term odor memory that brings back "remembrances of things past." Unlike this associative memory, sensory memory serves to monitor an unfamiliar or familiar odor in a certain environmental context within a relatively short time frame.

Sensory memory is an inherent factor in all psychophysical experience, but psychologists have generally ignored it. Some cognitive psychologists believe that a sensation is meaningless until it has been processed cognitively, but it seems to me that as soon as an odor is sensed it has a direct effect on behavior. King (1972) stresses the importance of remembering and monitoring sensations:

The substrate of all learned or adaptive behavior appears to rest on sense impressions that are directly apprehended. Rudimentary generalizations in behavior, based on events occurring in the environment or their sequence, may then—and only then—begin to arise. For this reason it is important to know far more than we now do about just how well sensory phenomena outlast the physical stimuli that give rise to them. (p. 245)

The natural function of the sense of smell is to provide information about the chemical environment. This assessment is usually done unconsciously, but when aroused by an odor, especially one that is unfamiliar, sniffing becomes a very vigorous and conscious activity. A familiar cooking odor from the kitchen will also be monitored and consciously noted occasionally to determine whether it might contaminate the air in the rest of the house. The degree to which the air is found annoying and its quality suspected determines the attention it receives. This applies to odors in the kitchen, stale air in the bedroom, suspected pollutants indoors and outdoors, and the odor of other people.

ODOR CONSTANCY

Smelling the ambient air is a natural routine. At the first hint of odor, the flow rate is increased by sniffing to bring the odor into focus for closer inspection. There is an optimum natural sniffing strength that delivers a volume of air of about 150cm^3 (Laing 1983). A weak sniff and a smaller volume decrease the perceived strength of a constant stimulus, but a stronger than natural sniff and a larger volume of air will not increase it significantly.

Sniffing has been simulated in the laboratory by making air flow through the nostrils at different rates, but it is interesting to note that such artificial and involuntary sniffing yields a different perceptual result from voluntary, self-regulated sniffing (Teghtsoonian, Teghtsoonian, Berglund, and Berglund 1978). Increasing the flow rate artificially makes an odor seem stronger, but perceived intensity remains constant when the flow rate is varied naturally by sniffing.

This constancy of perceptual intensity is analogous to a well-known visual phenomenon: Despite the fact that at different distances an object projects different sizes of images on the retina, the perceived size of the object remains unchanged. For the same reason, perceptual constancy of odors is required to adapt to the physical environment veridically, to keep track of a particular odor when other physical factors affect the perception of it.

After sniffing and sampling the air, an observer must decide whether it actually smells or not, and if so what the odor might be. Taking a number of standard sniffs improves the reliability of the judgment and aids in odor recognition and discrimination. At the same time, the control by sniffing tends to make exposure to the odorous atmosphere an intermittent rather than continuous stimulation, which helps prevent overexposure and fatigue.

KEEPING TRACK OF ODOR QUALITY

A common illustration of what is called short-term memory is holding a telephone number in mind between looking it up and dialing it. One can be easily distracted in this state and lose the information. It is likewise difficult to remember the name of a person to whom one has just been introduced at a party. It requires focusing attention on the name and actively keeping it in mind. The name can be transferred to long-term memory and thus used to advantage in the future. The ability to name odors is not as good, and therefore odor memory is less accurate than visual memory. At the same time, that is the reason why it is also more resistant to interference involving other odors and thus is less prone to distraction. The salient characteristic of odor perception is that it resists forgetting.

In a laboratory test of short-term memory (Engen, Kuisma, and Eimas 1973), an odor was first presented on a cotton swab to the subjects, who were told to keep it in mind. Then after a brief time interval either the inspected odor or a foil was presented, and the subject had to judge whether that odor was the same as the

Figure 4.1
Short-Term Odor Memory

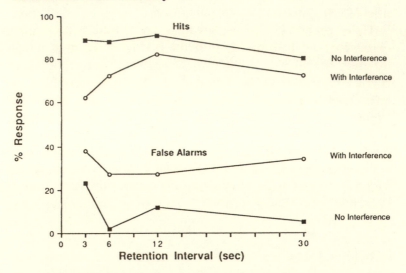

Note: Percent responses for various time intervals. Hits are correct identifications of the previously experienced odor quality. False alarms are incorrect judgments describing the foil, a different odor, as the same as the target.

target or different. The results are shown in Figure 4.1, which presents both hits—that is, correct affirmative responses—and false alarms (calling a foil "the same"). Overall, the accuracy is about 90 percent, with only a slight decrement for the longest retention interval.

In real life, of course, there is ordinarily competing stimulation that interferes with one's concentration on such a task. To simulate this mental noise, we required other subjects to count backward by threes, starting from some arbitrary number given to them just after they smelled the original odor. This interference makes the learning of the task more difficult, and performance is poorer from the beginning, but the interference does not cause forgetting. Being able to concentrate on only the odor is easier, but the distraction does not interfere with memory itself. The overall performance is a little poorer but still stable over time. The sense of smell is thus capable of keeping an odor in mind despite distraction.

These results are quite different from those of the classic experiment by Peterson and Peterson (1959) on memory for different trigrams of consonants, such as GKB and MRQ. A trigram was read to the subject with instructions that it be committed to memory. As soon as the subject had heard the trigram, he had to start counting backward by threes from an arbitrary number given by the experimenter. This prevented the subject from keeping the image of the trigram in mind by repeating the consonants to himself of by visualizing the trigram or representing it mentally in some other way. After a short period of time, a matter of seconds, the subject was asked to stop counting and repeat the trigram. Memory of trigrams was much better to begin with, but it was not as stable as odor memory is. The ability to recall a trigram decreases sharply, from about 80 percent after three seconds to 8 percent after only thirty seconds.

It has been suggested that the reason for the difference in results is that numbers do not interfere with odors as much as they do with letters. Intervening experience with other odors might be more detrimental to odor memory. To check this, subjects in another experiment had to inspect five different odorants but were tested for memory of only one of them. The average percentage of correct judgments of targets and foils for this group was poorer than in both of the other experiments with odor memory. Keeping the target odor in mind is now more difficult and that difficulty affects the overall performance, but there is still no evidence that the memory of the odor is fading over time.

Another interesting and characteristic result should be noted. Figure 4.1 shows that introducing the interfering task affects not so much the number of hits as the number of false alarms; that is, when the task gets harder because of interference, the subjects are more likely to describe a foil as the target. These errors increase to about 30 percent from the 10 percent level when there is no interference. Interference therefore affects the cognitive approach to the task and the judgment strategy rather than the strength of memory.

Remembering odors and verbal codes are quite different tasks. Unlike trigrams and names, odors are affected less by the passage of time. On the one hand, keeping an odor in mind is simpler because it does not require verbal monitoring, but on the other hand, odor memory does not have the advantage afforded by verbal encoding and thus is not as accurate as the memory of a trigram or a telephone number.

KEEPING TRACK OF A SERIES OF ODORS

The number of odors presented at one time affects the ability to retrieve each of them, and one would expect that the order in which they were experienced would affect memory. It is a well-established fact that the first and last members of a previously learned list of verbal items are better remembered than those in the middle (Wingfield and Byrnes 1981). The so-called primacy effect for the first item involves the greater opportunity to rehearse it, while the memory of the last item is better because it was seen more recently and thus is less likely to have faded away. An experiment conducted by Bruce M. Ross, Deborah Koenig, Amy Sisley, and me tested the effect of serial position with banana, clove, camphor, chocolate, citral, ginger, wintergreen, vanilla, and other common odors matched for strength. One odor was smelled after the other, with a short but definite pause between them, and serial position was indicated by the experimenter: "this is the first odor," "this is the second odor," and so forth. The subject had also been encouraged to label each odor, to help remember its serial position. When all twelve odors had been presented, odors were presented one at a time and the subjects were to identify the ordinal positions in the series. Different odors were tested with different subjects, so that all positions were tested equally often.

The results show that the subjects were correct about 40 percent of the time, with the first odor presented being remembered better (75 percent) than the rest. However, there is no evidence that an odor smelled most recently is better remembered than those smelled earlier. An even flatter function without any indication of a primacy effect was obtained by Gabassi and Zanuttini (1983) for pleasant floral and fruit odors, such as citral, eugenol, lemon, eucalyptus, and lavender. They point out that familiar odors that can be named, such as citral, are recognized better than unfamiliar ones (American mint was unfamiliar to Italian students). Thus, familiarity and better verbal encoding modify the effect of serial position.

To compare with visual data, we performed the same experiment with facial expressions of fear, happiness, disgust, surprise, anger, and other emotions displayed by an actress (Engen, Levy, and Schlosberg 1958). The results, which are presented in Figure 4.2, show a U-shaped function. There is a definite primacy effect, with perfect performance for the first four positions, as well as a recency effect, with perfect performance for the two last positions. The accuracy of judgments for the middle of the series dropped down to less than 40 percent at about the level of odors in ordinal positions seven and eight.

Another noticeable difference between visual and odor recognition is that memory of odors is poorer overall than that of pictures. The reason more errors are made with odors than with faces probably is the poorer ability to name odors—to associate odors with verbal labels that will help to retrieve them from memory later on (Engen 1987). Obviously, being able to identify an item verbally makes the task easier. Facial expressions are easily described, and one can mentally repeat these descriptions to oneself—for example, "disgust," "fear," "remorse," and so on as a new one, "happiness," is added. Lack of such semantic mnemonic aids impairs the performance in this kind of test of odor memory, but by the same token, odor memory does not suffer from the interference among names and labels, which results in the U-shaped function for pictures. In general, memory of different odors is more even.

Figure 4.2
The Effect of Serial Position on Memory

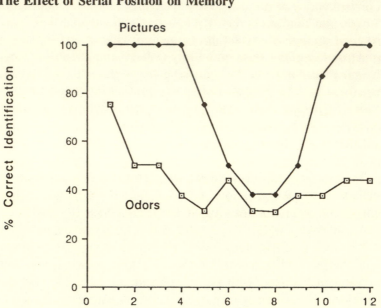

Serial Position of Test Item

Note: Percent correct judgments of the ordinal position of items in a previously
experienced series for pictures of the facial expression of emotions and
for odors.

KEEPING TRACK OF ODOR INTENSITY

Memory Span

It has been shown that humans can keep in mind more than a
dozen different sweet and fruity odors at one time (Engen and
Pfaffman 1960). The question here is what the memory span is
for different intensities of one odor: For example, is it possible
to keep in mind five strengths of lemon odor at the same time?

In one experiment we varied the number of different intensities (concentrations of n-butanol) that the subjects were to memorize (Engen and Pfaffmann 1959). They first compared side by side the odor strength of each of the distinctly different concentrations to learn to associate strength with rank order—the strongest, next strongest, and so forth. To test memory, each concentration was then presented in random order, and the subject's task was to identify the rank order. The results show clearly that memory for different odor intensities includes at best only four categories and that this kind of attention span is poorer for odors than for other sensory attributes such as the loudness of a tone. Other modalities, according to Miller (1956), conform to the famous rule of seven plus or minus two. One reason for the difference is the difficulty of associating odors with a code.

A Target Odor

The environmental and practical problem, however, is more often to identify what one odor is and then to monitor its strength. The following anecdotal evidence illustrates the central problem of this chapter. In the middle of the night one is awakened by what sounds like wheels spinning, tires burning on the pavement, and cars racing up the street. Later one becomes aware of an odor that seems to fit that hypothesis, but there is doubt. Perhaps something—an electric wire—is burning in the house. Aroused and now fully awake, one sniffs the air at intervals to determine whether or not the odor is increasing or decreasing, comparing the memory of the sensation from the first sample of it. Satisfied that the odor is getting weaker and that it came from outside, one puts it out of mind and goes back to sleep.

In a study of this ability to keep track of an odor's strength, subjects were asked to identify a previously experienced odor (a 25 percent solution of n-butanol). Some subjects were given a number immediately after sniffing the odor and were required to count backward from it by threes to prevent them from concentrating on the odor. Other subjects were tested after a

Figure 4.3
Memory of Odor Strength

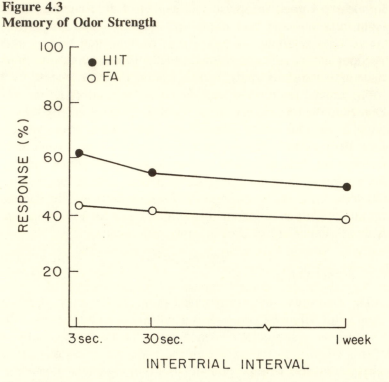

Note: Percent responses after various intervals of time between the initial experience of and the test of memory odors of various strength. Hits are correct identifications. False alarms are incorrect judgments describing a weaker or stronger foil as the same as the target.

short pause with either the original odor or a stronger or weaker foil. The task was to judge whether the second odor was the same as or different from the target. Still other subjects were tested with either the target, the stronger foil, or the weaker foil after one week.

There were two noteworthy findings. The first, as shown in Figure 4.3, is that although performance was relatively poor, the subjects selected the correct intensity more often than not. Keep in mind that this is a difficult laboratory test, and that it is not clear how well it represents a real-life task. However, once again, odor memory was stable, remaining at about 60 percent for all three intervals. Accuracy was poor, as indicated by the high percentage of false alarms, although no more errors were made after the short intervals than were made after a week.

The second interesting finding was an asymmetry in the responses to the foils, which is not revealed by the averages shown in this graph. One would expect that errors would as often involve weak as strong foils, but in fact there were more false alarms with the stronger foils than with the weaker ones. In other words, the weaker foils were more likely to be correctly rejected as different, while the stronger foils tended to be misidentified as the target. This nonrandom distribution of errors indicates that there is a tendency to remember the target as stronger than it really is. Such a bias reflects a general attitude which I think is characteristic of odor perception, a bias that is also reflected in the choice of verbal response categories used to describe odors: One finds that odors are more often categorized as "strong" or "pungent" than "weak" or "bland."

OTHER MODALITIES

A high percentage of false alarms is characteristic of odor perception, but the tendency to describe stimuli as strong rather than weak is not. A number of experiments have been performed involving similar tasks in other modalities. For example, one may present a nonmusical sound of a certain pitch and loudness and later ask the subject to reproduce it by manipulating the frequency and intensity. Or the experimenter may draw a line that the subject is required to reproduce with a pencil on a piece of paper following the lapse of different periods of time. Variations of this task with retention intervals ranging from seconds to weeks have been performed in the study of some two dozen different sensory attributes, and all the tests have had similar results (King 1972; Alin 1986).

Human subjects can reproduce such simple physical stimuli with good accuracy, but when they err it is by setting the stimulus to be larger than the target. This overestimation has been interpreted as support for the so-called consolidation theory of memory, according to which the trace strengthens in time as factors interfering with the items to be memorized weaken. However, I believe that it reflects a general response bias, a worry about overstimulation, and a feature of the central control that assesses environmental stimulation by erring on the side of safety. What is different about odor perception is the nature of the errors, the tendency toward false alarms.

The practical problems of how odors are monitored are not easily observed in the laboratory, but the data show that humans can readily cope, as they must, in the real world. For relatively short timespans memory is poorer for odors than for pictures. However, once an odor is encoded in memory, it is not affected as much by distractions as visual images are. Not only do odors persist through extensive exposure (see Chapter 3) but they also resist interference from the input of other information.

The possibility of encountering such interference naturally increases with the passage of time. Freedom from it is perhaps the primary reason that odor memory is so timeless. Thus, the results presented here show that how recently a stimulus was presented is a strong factor for visual memory but does not really affect odor memory.

5

Smells

An odor may cause either approach or avoidance, and this is not just another way of describing pleasant and unpleasant odors. An odor need not have unpleasant sensory attributes to cause annoyance or stress, as we noted in Chapter 2 in discussing the arousal value of unfamiliar odors. This chapter discusses unidentified odors and contexts in which odors contribute to unpleasant experiences with negative effects.

THE PERCEPTION OF POLLUTION

Individual Differences

If one samples the opinions of a reasonably large group of people, any odor is likely to be judged quite differently from the majority by some individuals. In one experiment (Engen and McBurney 1964), for example, all but one of forty subjects found guaiacol, obtained from hardwood tar and used as an antiseptic, to be more or less unpleasant, but one person liked it very much; it reminded him of happy days on Cape Cod, where his mother had used a household cleaning product with that odor. Most find the odor of hydrogen sulfide ("rotten eggs") to be obnoxious, but some like it because of its association with the seaside. To some workers in pulp mills it smells like money (Third Karolinska Institute Symposium on Environmental Health, 1970).

Perception of Control

In addition to previous experience with it, another factor determining the response to an odor is the extent to which one feels able to control the odor. This is an important topic in environmental psychology generally (Bell, Fisher, Baum, and Greene 1990). People are better able to cope with an adverse environmental condition when they believe they can do something about it. Just to understand the source of the problem appears to be beneficial. Being stuck in a boring and physically stressful job controlled by a noncommunicative and arbitrary boss is psychologically unhealthy.

An unknown odor, whether real or imagined, will be assumed to be harmful in such relentlessly adverse circumstances. In more than half of some two dozen documented cases of mass hysteria, a strange unidentified odor played a major role (Colligan and Murphy 1982). In each of these cases, large numbers of people became sick with symptoms of nausea, dizziness, fainting, and apparent irritation of eyes and throat; they attributed these symptoms to odor, although no toxic agent could be found to correlate with them. The odor was frequently described as strange but not unpleasant. This situation shows how the impact of an odor is not predetermined by properties inherent in it but how its impact depends on the context in which it is perceived. This includes perfume. If a person believes that it is being used to influence him, he might actually find it disagreeable (Baron 1988).

Odor Motivation

If an odor is not recognized it will be perceived as potentially harmful. The reason is not because of the sensory attributes of the odor, whether pleasant or unpleasant, but because the odor's source is unknown. The "sick building syndrome" or "tight building syndrome" is a case in point. In addition to irritation of eyes and skin, dizziness, and headaches, it often involves the experience of a persistent unidentified odor. Some people believe that this syndrome is a psychosomatic or psychogenic problem and that it is not "real" because no chemical cause has been identified. However, the syndrome is similar to that caused by exposure to formaldehyde, which may be emitted from various modern construction materials for extended periods of time. A known carcinogen, formaldehyde irritates the mucus membranes and the respiratory system and has a persistent pungent odor that causes constant arousal and annoyance. There are many chemicals in the indoor air (Berglund, Berglund, Lindvall, and Nicander-Bredberg 1982; Johansson 1990), and many have not yet been identified by modern technology. Because of its greater sensitivity, the human sense of smell may detect these chemicals when mechanical detection devices fail to do so.

A general hypothesis in social psychology, the Byrne-Clore reinforcement-affect model (1970), describes the negative influence of degraded environments on interpersonal relationships. A person will be judged less attractive in a smelly, crowded, and stuffy atmosphere. In one study the ratings of attractiveness of other people were found to be lower if the classroom in which the ratings were made was pervaded by the rancid odor of butyric acid or the rotten odor of ammonium sulfide (Rotton, Barry, Frey, and Soler 1978).

Within this general theoretical framework, odors have been used to change unhealthy eating and drinking habits in behavior modification therapy. The assumption is that such odors are unconditional stimuli, which when paired with a favorite dessert or drink will make it undesirable (Foreyt and Kennedy 1971).

However, although some odors—skunk for example—may be disliked by most people, they are not really unconditional but conditional stimuli. They are not analogous to the meat in the presence of which Pavlov's dog naturally salivated; rather, they are like the bell to whose sound the dog learned to salivate. It should be borne in mind that some people actually like skunk odor because of special individual experiences. In other words, preference and its effect on behavior are not inherent in the odor but are acquired. Knowledge of a patient's odor experiences might be used to advantage in selecting odors for behavior modification therapy. An odor to which a patient has acquired an aversion may act like an unconditional stimulus in changing responses that are otherwise difficult to extinguish or unlearn.

THE PSYCHOPHYSIOLOGY OF ODOR PERCEPTION

Bodily State

Tobacco, alcohol, and other chemical substances affect bodily state, well-being, and performance separately and together. One of our experiments was concerned with their effect on odor perception (Engen 1986c). It tested the ability of healthy young adults under the influence of alcohol and carbon monoxide to detect a smoky odor (guaiacol). The alcohol dose, which was determined by the individual's weight, was enough vodka in orange juice to produce a blood alcohol level of 7.6 mg/ml, just under the legal limit for driving. The amount of carboxyhemoglobin in the blood was elevated in the subjects to a level similar to that of a pack-a-day smoker (6–8 g/ml) by having them inhale carefully monitored air containing carbon monoxide.

There were two interesting results. First, contrary to expectation, test performance was actually better when the subjects were under the influence of either alcohol or carbon monoxide separately. For alcohol, a popular explanation for this improvement in acuity is psychological disinhibition; that is, alcohol relaxes a person and thus improves performance in the simple detection task. This explanation does not seem to apply to the increase in sensitivity by carbon monoxide, but there is another possible explanation applicable to both agents. The increased sensitivity could have been due to arousal. A small amount of either chemical will cause an initial defensive reaction, which in turn leads to more careful monitoring of sensory signals. Alcohol may first cause arousal and then disinhibition. This indirect influence of arousal on performance is supported by closer analysis of the odor detection performance.

Second, the chemicals did not really affect odor sensitivity. Instead, they caused a change in the strategy for interpreting sensory input, which is evident as a decrease in the number of false alarms. The hit rate—that is, correct judgments of the presence of odor—was actually the same across these various drug conditions.

Potentiation

Larger amounts of either alcohol or carbon monoxide would naturally have adverse effects, but only one low level of each could be tested in this experiment. However, subjects' detection performance was poorer when they were exposed to both agents simultaneously. But again, the effect was observed not on odor sensitivity but on performance. The result now was an increase in the number of false alarms. Smoking and drinking potentiate each other's harmful effects if taken together, but the effect on perception is only indirect.

The interaction of different factors in performance is a general problem. Failure to take it into account may be the reason that studies of the effect of low levels of carbon monoxide on various kinds of human performance have had inconsistent results. Agents such as drugs or simple fatigue, which are inconsequential by themselves, may have potentiated the effects of a low level of other agents. The standard approach to environmental control of merely specifying maximum allowable exposures to substances separately is of limited practical value. (See also the discussion of facilitation in Chapter 3.)

The same applies to the understanding of odors and their strength. Ordinarily, odors from different sources do not simply add arithmetically (Cain and Drexler 1974). Adding a second odor to a strong one hardly makes any difference (Berglund, 1990). A mixture of two odors usually tends to be weaker than expected from the perceived strength of each singly, but in some cases one odor may potentiate another and act synergistically. Methods for analyzing interactions of environmental stimuli need to be developed to a higher and more sophisticated level.

SOURCES OF MALODOR

Odors Outdoors

Odorous air pollutants are usually mixtures of different chemicals. In one large city in Florida, according to the *Providence Sunday Journal*, "the combined odor of the airport, a brewery, two pulp mills, a chemical plant and the city sewage treatment plant prevents it from being a world-class city." Such extreme cases elicit many complaints to the authorities and attention by the media. The frequency of spontaneous complaints about odorous pollution is as great as that of complaints about noise pollution (Third Karolinska Institute Symposium on Environmental Health, 1970). The number of complaints is highest for central heating plants, followed by sanitary stations or dumps; facilities for processing food; textile, thread, leather, and rubber factories; mechanical shops and steel plants; tanneries; cement, limestone, asphalt, and stone processing facilities; and cellulose and paper plants.

It is not known objectively what makes some odors, such as diesel fumes, seem worse than others. People appear to find the odor of cows and horses much more acceptable than that of most other animals, for reasons that are not obvious. More than mere sensation is involved. Visible signs of pollution, such as soot, dust, and other particulates, make an ambient odor seem more pungent (Engen 1972). Meteorological conditions are important; for example, all odors are stronger, more toxic, and more unpleasant downwind of their source. Odors from unknown sources will get attention, and it is noteworthy that industry is steadily producing more and more new products that smell.

Indoor Air

Although outdoor odor pollution may get more attention from the press, indoor pollution may be worse. The fact that people spend much more time indoors than outdoors accentuates the problem. In the 1930s health officials in the state of New York began research using odor as the index by which to judge the quality of indoor air (Yaglou, Riley, and Coggins 1936).

More recent studies of schools and offices conducted by the Environmental Protection Agency and by various research groups have found that there are over 200 aromatics, halogens, esters, alcohols, phenols, ethers, ketones, aldehydes, epoxides, and aliphatic hydrocarbons in public indoor areas (Berglund, Berglund, Lindvall, and Nicander-Bredburg 1982). There are still other odorous pollutants that current methodology (e.g., gas chromatography and flame ionization detection) has not been able to identify. The home environment is no better; in fact, it is often worse. Fresh air for ventilation is contaminated when it passes through dirty filters or, because of poor design, through other rooms of a building rather than coming directly from outdoors. The numbers of potential pollutants exceed those for the outdoor air; they include additional pollutants from building materials, carpets, cooking facilities, heating fuels, various deodorants and cleaning products, and all kinds of modern vinyls and plastics.

The odors associated with modern construction materials are now foremost in the public mind, but historically tobacco and body odor were considered the main culprits. The goal of some of the pioneering experiments in the 1930s was to determine the amount of fresh air needed in a room to make it odor free (Yaglou, Riley, and Coggins 1936). The motivation then was to alleviate annoyance rather than to protect health, as it is today. To study the effect of the odor of tobacco smoke, for example, Yaglou placed a small group of people in an airtight room in which ventilation could be controlled precisely. The occupants smoked a certain number of cigarettes over a specified period of time under various levels of ventilation. The strength of the odor was then rated on a four-point scale of slight, moderate, strong, or very strong by a panel of judges who briefly visited the room. (Modern research chambers have "sniffing ports," which allow better experimental control of the air to be sampled and the judges' perceptual task.)

Yaglou and his colleagues tested the strength of body odors with the same method. People were kept in a nonventilated room; the more people and the longer they occupied the room, the stronger the odor became. The goal was to determine how much fresh air was needed to reduce body or tobacco odors to an acceptable level.

The amount of carbon dioxide in the air correlates with the perceived strength of odors, and this chemical was therefore used as an objective index of indoor air quality to supplement human judgments. (Carbon dioxide, which is odorless, increases as oxygen is used up and the air becomes contaminated.) To be acceptable, it was determined, the air must contain no more than 0.15 percent by volume of carbon dioxide. About one-third of the air in the room may have to be changed every minute, Yaglou concluded, to maintain quality according to this standard.

The complexity of this problem, involving the number and kind of occupants (children smell stronger than adults) and the nature of other sources of odors, has prevented researchers from reaching a consensus on a precise formula for air exchange. What is clear, however, is that a lot of fresh air is required to keep a room odorless, an expensive proposition. That was not a problem in the 1930s when fuel was cheap. The attempt to save energy in the 1970s led to the construction of tight but "sick" buildings.

One problem involves the length of time that an odor lingers. Different pollutants require more time and more fresh air to disperse than others. It seems that the worse the pollutant, the more time is required to get rid of it. At one extreme, years may be required to get rid of the odor of construction materials in a modern building. Tobacco odor can persist for days after the smoking in a room has ceased. By contrast, body odor will dissipate relatively quickly and will be reduced to an acceptable level in a matter of minutes.

Odor control technology has concentrated on the detection of individual pollutants, but no objective index of air quality has been obtained. Although, as we have seen, there is a correlation between unhealthy air and the presence of carbon dioxide, it is merely a correlation, a rough index, which does not account for or explain odor. Tobacco smoke alone contains literally thousands of chemicals. While the overall odor strength increases with the number of odorous chemicals in the air (Berglund, Berglund, Lindvall, and Nicander-Bredburg 1982), the ways in which such chemicals add up and interact pose unsolved mathematical, chemical, and perceptual problems. It is curious that progress in the technology of heating and ventilation engineering has not been matched by developments in odor control technology.

Not all chemicals are odorous, including such highly toxic ones as carbon monoxide, but contaminated air usually contains a number of different chemicals, some of which will be odorous. Thus the best index of air quality is odor, and the sense of smell is still the most sensitive and versatile instrument for judging air quality. Better than any other sensor, it is fairly robust (see Chapter 2) and not as easily distracted as has been claimed on the basis of some unrealistic laboratory experiments (Whisman, Goetzinger, Cotton, and Brinkman 1978).

This human instrument is also useful in other areas, even when mechanical detection devices are available. Fish odor provides one interesting example. Japanese researchers have proposed that a sensor be built to test the freshness of fish. Ambient concentrations of trimethylamine and ammonia gases produced in deteriorating muscle tissue can be measured chemically (*Science News*, 29 October 1988, p. 287), but not with the speed and sensitivity of the human nose. The Food and Drug Administration still uses trained observers to judge the acceptability of fish by its odor (see Engen 1982), and the use of human observers for similar purposes is actually increasing (Fanger 1988).

Use of the sense of smell takes advantage of its sensitivity to low concentrations and versatility in being able to detect diverse odor qualities. The measurement of odor pollution is, of course, first of all a human psychophysical problem. Better techniques of chemical analysis may be developed in the future, but the human sense of smell will remain an irreplaceable instrument in the perception of odor pollution.

DEODORIZATION

Masking

Instead of adding fresh air, a more common and possibly less expensive method of increasing the pleasantness of a room is by perfuming it. This is a psychological technique involving masking or modulating one odor with another. Not only the air but consumer products such as women's stockings, pillows, and the like are perfumed to make them more attractive. Both outdoor and indoor air affect the price of real estate, and it is recommended that in preparing a house for sale you should "smell it before you sell it," eliminating all odors from cooking, pets, mildew, and medicines by covering them with various scents such as fresh latex paint, carpet shampoo, lemony waxes, freesia flowers, and freshly baked bread.

However, there is a limit to the effectiveness of masking. The present state of the art is limited despite the promise on the labels of deodorizer containers that the contents will improve the air by "absorbing and neutralizing malodors." (I am not referring to modification of one ingredient by another in a liquid solution.) A pleasant odor can hide a malodor in a room, but only when the malodor is relatively weak. Adding a fragrance to a strong malodor will not eliminate it but may in fact amplify it. Consider the following example from the bathroom in an apartment I once rented. The plumbing of the drainpipes allowed toilet odors to escape into the bathroom through an open drain in the floor. With regular flushing this would not necessarily have happened. However, the apartment had been vacant for some time, and the bathroom had a very bad sewer smell. The remedy tried by my wife was to attach a deodorizer on the wall near the drain. By itself this deodorizer emitted a nice floral odor, but unfortunately, not only did it not mask the malodor, it actually increased it. One could now smell both odors, and the combination was decidedly unpleasant. The sewer odor seemed stronger and therefore worse than before, and the floral odor had an added attribute of sewer. The solution was to wait patiently for time, water, and fresh air to do the job.

Artificial Odors

When possible, it is best to avoid use of artificial odors, which make the environment olfactorily "noisy." Even when a deodorizer helps, it is not good for the simple reason that if the air smells it is contaminated and should be cleaned. That is what is wrong with the old practice of using perfumes to cover up body odors. One should be aware of dirt and contamination. Suppose, to take another example, a method was perfected to eliminate the perception of the odor of cigarette smoke. It would benefit restaurant owners and others who want to satisfy smokers as well as nonsmokers, but it would expose the public to a very large number of odorless agents in tobacco smoke (Raab 1987).

Of course, the use of a small amount of perfume to make the air smell better is hardly a matter of risk. Likewise, covering up the chemical odors of women's stockings, shaving preparations, shampoos, and other products can be done safely. However, there is not only a physical limit to the value of masking odors, as I have just described, but there is a psychological one as well. What is perfume to one person may be unfamiliar and therefore a negative stimulus to another. One must know in advance or be told that an odor in a strange place is a perfume, because the ability to identify the source of odors with the sense of smell is poor. Finally, I disagree with claims that odors have inherent motivational and emotional effects; for example, that fragrances such as lemon delivered through air-conditioning ducts can stimulate worker productivity. That is the topic of the next chapter on pleasant odors.

6

Fragrances and Perfumes

Sensory pleasure and psychological benefits are thought to accrue to fragrances and perfumes. Fragrances have traditionally been associated with herbal and folk medicine and the belief that odors have healing effects. Perfumes were originally used to mask or modify malodors with pleasant odors. Although the two terms are frequently used interchangeably, I use *perfume* to refer to commercial products concocted from many ingredients and *fragrance* to refer to natural products of vegetable origin.

There are three kinds of ingredients found in perfumes: various chemical compounds, so-called essential oils, and certain animal products. The last category includes musk from the abdomen of the small musk deer; castoreum, a creamy substance from the pineal gland of the beaver; civet from a pouch near the sexual organ of the civet cat; and ambergris, a fatty substance from the digestive system of whales. These ingredients serve two purposes in perfumes. First, they provide a foundation, or fixative, to make the whole mixture physically and perceptually stable so that it will last without change in quality. Second, these animal products, especially musk, have been assumed to have the power to arouse sexual feelings and motivation.

Fragrances and perfumes are commonly employed to manipulate interpersonal relations and to cure psychiatric problems. Fragrances used for these purposes are mainly essential oils obtained from the blossoms, stems, seeds, bark, roots, and leaves of a variety of plants by extraction, distillation, enfleurage, or pressing. Synthetics produced by chemists, who can copy the makeup of natural odorants, are often used as substitutes. The quality of synthetics is steadily increasing, and they are produced at a lower cost and with fewer impurities than are natural odorants.

All perfumes contain many ingredients. A given perfume might contain the essential oils of rose, citrus blossoms, lavender, sandalwood, and many other plants, plus ordinary chemicals such as coumarin from coal tar. The blend of all these ingredients will be combined with animal products or synthetics to prevent the more volatile oils from evaporating too quickly and altering the perceptual quality of the odor. The resulting concentrate of some twenty-five or more different ingredients is then diluted in alcohol and is presented in a concentration of about 10 to 25 percent as a perfume and about 4 percent as a cologne.

Clearly, it is not easy to isolate the effects of fragrances, because each essential oil is not a simple chemical compound but consists of so many different substances. Nevertheless, odor therapists describe quite specifically how they think fragrances affect people, and for that reason odor therapy provides a clear example for the present topic. It contrasts with my view that the effects of fragrances depend on the context in which they are experienced.

THEORIES OF ODOR THERAPY

Aroma Therapy

Aroma therapy is an old practice that recently has gained renewed popularity. Its central hypothesis is that the odor of natural products—of "Mother Nature"—can cure psychological problems. Rovesti and Colombo (1973), two of its more recent champions, trace its history to French and Italian herbalists of the 1930s. They maintain that some essential oils, including geraniol, menthol, and camphor, are sedatives and that others, such as eugenol, thymol, and citral, are stimulants.

Specific fragrances are thus recommended for specific mental therapies. Depression can be treated with the odors of lemons and oranges. Myrtle, mint, and sage can prevent an attack of epilepsy. Anxiety can be relieved by neroli and lavender, and tension by freesia and freshly cut hay. Valerian oil is a sedative serving as an antidote to migraine headaches and insomnia. Mixtures of essential oils can be used for an individual patient's special problems.

Success is also claimed for using odors to soothe the pains associated with toothache, to stimulate the intellectual faculties, and even to counteract the adverse psychological effects of malodors. Rovesti and Colombo describe experiments in tanning factories and chemical plants where they successfully used various aerosols containing the essential oils of water-mint, verbena, and lavender as antidotes to malodors. They report that these fragrances changed the workers' mental state and that productivity increased by 10 to 15 percent.

Aerosol presentation is recommended in such cases because it offers the advantages of uniform diffusion, ease of dosage control, and natural experience of the essential oil in "ambient olfaction" (Rovesti and Colombo, 1973, p. 477). The procedures in individual cases are different. In treating anxiety, for example, it is recommended that three times daily a lump of sugar with about two drops of valerian be placed on the patient's tongue and that the patient inhale the vapors while the lump slowly dissolves. For sleep and relaxation, camomile, geraniums, hollyhocks, orange blossoms, and mint prepared in a tea or tisane are recommended.

Massage is another important vehicle. Good therapeutic results, it is claimed, can be obtained by using massage oil scented with the proper essential oils. Mixtures in which each ingredient is to produce a particular effect are often used (Rovesti and Colombo, 1973, p. 476). However, a strong odor from a single essential oil may be used with great effect in certain cases, according to Tisserand (1988), a leading aroma therapist, who relates the following anecdote from a colleague:

My patient was suffering from acute depression. During the treatment he became convinced he was floating in the air, and kept opening his eyes, fearing he was about to bang his head on the ceiling. I barely finished the massage when I had to crawl to the nearest floor space where I "passed out." I came to an hour later and woke my patient with some coffee. The treatment was totally successful, and he left somewhat high and ethereal. When I work out some form of mask to wear, I might consider using clary sage again! (p. 176)

The reason for the effects of fragrances, aroma therapists believe, is that they act on the psychosomatic roots of mental problems. The therapists claim that in the right doses, fragrances are harmless "nerve oils" without the side effects of ordinary drugs taken internally. The fragrances' effects are transmitted via the olfactory nerves to the limbic system, where emotional behavior and odor interact.

Although only clinical anecdotes are reported by aroma therapists, the effects on the brain of different fragrances have been observed with electroencephalographs (Torii et al. 1988) and with measurements of other responses of cortical activity (Van Toller 1988). In particular, jasmine is said to have stimulating and lavender sedative effects in such records of brain activity, but no specific neural activities or brain locations have been isolated.

Aroma therapists believe that for an odor to be effective it must have a natural source. There is a vitalism, or "life force," implied in this view of the chemical nature of stimuli and their effects. The odors cannot be synthetic. This is a salient difference between aroma therapy and other kinds of odor therapy that use both synthetics and natural essential oils. An exchange between a manufacturer of fragrances and an aroma therapist that took place at a conference on the psychology and biology of perfumes illustrates this point (Van Toller and Dodd, 1988). The manufacturer challenged the aroma therapist with the following question: "If one matches an essential oil synthetically so that the odors of the natural product and the synthetic one are indistinguishable to human observers, would the synthetic then have the therapeutic effect of the essential oil?" The response of the aroma therapist was guarded but clearly in the negative.

Considering their claims to the efficacy of their treatments, aroma therapists are open to a potentially disturbing question. If fragrances are used like drugs, both those who produce them and those who use them may be legally responsible for their effects.

Osmotherapy

Like aroma therapists, osmotherapists believe that the psychological effect of an odor is mediated by the limbic system. However, they reject both the vitalism of aroma therapy and its hypothesis that only natural products will work. Dodd (1988), who is a perfume chemist and an osmotherapist, does believe that odors have therapeutic effects, but he states that "I have in my perfumery practice used the *odours* both of exotic natural perfume oils and new, unusual, synthetic materials in helping people to relax" (p. 30). And while aroma therapists make only a general reference to the nervous system, osmotherapists are searching for "perfume molecules" and their sites and "perfume receptors" in the peripheral nervous system.

Resolution of the argument about synthetic versus natural odors, according to Dodd, would require the ability to observe what takes place neurologically, beginning at the peripheral level, where odorous molecules interact with receptors. He proposes determining whether fragrances with similar effects on people might, for example, have common stereochemical structures or other common characteristics by which they could be systematically categorized. Osmotherapy provides an example of traditional reductionism and its search for specific odors and their receptors that are expected to provide explanations for the different effects of different fragrances. But its adherents have not yet been able to identify inherent stimulating properties of odors or show how they are connected with the innervation of the limbic system and emotions (Van Toller 1988).

Relaxation Therapy

So-called enhanced relaxation therapy uses odor experience as an auxiliary for the reduction of anxiety (King 1988). Sensory stimuli associated with relaxation—such as the odor of "the seaside" together with sounds of waves, wind, and birds—can be presented simultaneously for a realistic effect. The special contribution of odor is its evocative nature, which is assumed to be more effective than, for example, having a patient concentrate on a single word (mantra) as used in meditation. Odors are said to be better in this regard than visual images, which are likely to entail idiosyncratic sensory associations—such as the color of a bathing suit worn on the beach—not shared by the patient and the therapist.

King acknowledges the ecological attributes of odor: "The psychological effect of a fragrance is highly dependent on the context in which it is encountered" (p. 157). However, it is curious that he does not think that memory plays any role in this therapy. It seems to me that the effects of particular milieu concepts such as the seaside by definition involve learning, memory, and the whole brain. A liking for the odor of the seaside is clearly acquired. For relaxation therapy, the best odors, I think, are those associated with pleasant experiences, such as the feeling of comfort and nurturing associated with a patient's mother's body odor. Such stimuli, as we have seen earlier, most nearly resemble unconditional stimuli.

The Limbic System

According to all the theories we have been examining, odor stimulation activates the limbic system and a related circuitry of emotion and motivation. Two important assumptions are made.

One is that odor control is bottom-up, that is there is central brain control of the effect of odor stimulation. The other is that the limbic system integrates all the effects of odor stimulation with both hormonal effects and environmental experiences with odors. In short, the limbic system is believed to be "the smell brain" (see, for example, Van Toller and Dodd 1988).

However, the limbic system cannot be claimed to be specialized for odor perception. This system of the central brain includes cortical structures, such as the hippocampus, as well as subcortical parts of the brain—including, for example, the amygdala and the hypothalamus, which have many other functions (Swanson 1987). It is connected to all parts of the nervous system, receiving direct input not only from the olfactory bulb but also from other modalities. The limbic system does not only or even primarily serve olfaction and "what we feel," but rather various cognitive functions of "what we know," including memory. Swanson suggests that the very term *limbic system* may have outlived its usefulness. A still stronger argument can be made against thinking of it as "the smell brain."

Stimulus Control

There is yet another problem pertaining to the neural and associated healing effects of fragrances. It is still not known what happens to chemical molecules in the nostrils, where the response to a fragrance is initiated. In addition to odor sensation this may cause other effects. It is also not known what happens to these molecules after they have stimulated the olfactory receptors. A common assumption is that they are eliminated like other waste products or neutralized by so-called detoxification enzymes (*Science News* 1989) and that they have no further biological effect.

However, at least some fragrances might both stimulate olfactory receptors and enter the bloodstream via the nasal passages, like drugs taken internally. (Using the nose, in fact, is becoming an increasingly popular method for drug administration; there is more to that than the illicit use of cocaine.) Thus, taking a fragrance in a lump of sugar or being massaged with essential oils may involve drug effects on systems other than olfaction. Those who use fragrances for therapeutic and other motivational effects generally fail to make this distinction, and the interpretation of their results may therefore be invalid. This applies to the use of perfume as well, which we will now examine.

THE PERSONAL USES OF PERFUME

Impression Management

A common reason for using perfume is to create a favorable impression on other people, a device that Baron (1988) describes as the art of impression management. Smelling good is expected to induce positive responses from others when one is applying for a job, selling a product, or contributing to a decision at a committee meeting. According to this view, one should not only dress properly for the occasion but wear the right kind of perfume in order to convey the right message. Different perfumes are considered to be appropriate for a business meeting and an evening at a single's bar. Such are the messages conveyed by the perfume industry's advertisements.

Baron and his students conducted a number of experiments to determine the effect of perfume in business situations. The men who served as subjects believed that the study involved their assessment of others' performances in job interviews and did not know that they themselves were the subjects and that the real purpose was to assess the effects of perfumes on them. They were asked to interview women who were—unknown to them, of course—accomplices of the experimenters. Two factors were manipulated. One was odor. Half of the interviewees wore no perfume at all, while the other half wore one of several common commercial perfumes. The other factor studied in the experiment was clothing. Half of the women were dressed informally in jeans, and the other half were dressed more formally, in skirts, blouses, and hose. After the interviews, the subjects were asked to rate each woman on how well they liked her.

The main finding was that the effect of the perfume depended on how the women were dressed. When they were dressed formally the perfume made them seem less attractive, but when they were dressed in jeans they seemed warmer and more romantic. Questioning the subjects afterward revealed that because in the college setting the more informal dress would be appropriate, the combination of formal dress and perfume made the women seem conceited. In other words, the situation determined the response to the perfume, not the reverse. The perception of perfume is not the result of simple olfactory stimulation; perfume is evaluated in context, consciously or unconsciously.

In another similar experiment, the reactions of men and women were compared. The effect of a popular perfume, one for each gender, was tested and compared with wearing no perfume. The interviewees were again asked questions about career plans and about their interactions with other people. After the interviews, the subjects provided recommendations regarding hiring and the potential success of each "job candidate" based on appearance and attractiveness as well as personality characteristics such as intelligence and warmth.

The results showed an interesting gender difference. Male subjects typically rated the candidates lower but female subjects rated them higher when they had used perfume than when they had not. Baron speculates that men perceive the use of perfume as part of an attempt to impress or manipulate them. If the interviewee acted too friendly or even coquettish, the effect of perfume might become even more negative, producing "too much of a good thing," according to Baron. Women, on the other hand, are generally more comfortable around perfume and are thus able to "filter out" the fragrance factor in judging the interviewee.

Fragrances do have a stimulating effect in keeping the environment interesting and counteracting boredom. The attention-getting and evocative attributes of odors may play a crucial role in keeping our minds alert and engaged. Yet the contexts in which fragrances are used for environmental or personal management must be clearly defined to take advantage of this, because the responses to fragrances are not predetermined by the fragrances' attributes. Indeed, perfume may have the opposite effect from the one intended by its user.

Self-Esteem

Perfume is a luxury item associated with money and status. Le Norcy (1988) points out that perfumes were originally used by wealthy Parisians, who had their own special perfumes created for them. Perfumes are now within the reach of most consumers, and they are rarely custom creations, but the association with money and success remains. Some feel that perfumes help build their self-image and self-esteem. Byrne-Quinn (1988) writes that using perfume is both an aesthetic experience and a part of "the ritual of 'getting ready,' whether for an evening out or in bed" (p. 206). Perfume, she suggests, helps build up confidence that one will do well socially. These interesting ideas are based on opinion polling rather than experimentation, and actually involve complex relationships between many factors. The data do not reveal the specific contribution of the perfume itself. The causal link is not clear, and it has certainly not been demonstrated that perfumes produce social skills and self-esteem, as research often supported by the fragrance industry tends to imply.

Many people claim that odors, and in particular what they consider good perfumes, affect them profoundly and in a special way. This is a reason, they say, for paying a good deal of money for a perfume. Gordon Shepherd (1988), a well-known neuroscientist specializing in olfaction, believes that the experience of a good perfume is analogous to the mental state that

T. S. Eliot, in "The Dry Savages," describes as "music heard so deeply" that it transcends mere physical auditory stimulation.

THE ROLE OF EXPERIENCE

A fragrance may capture one's mind with an experience that transcends mere sensory stimulation and arousal through its associations with other events. It is through personal experiences of this kind that fragrances obtain warmth and sensuality. Pictures of people and scenes can also stimulate one's imagination, but such images are pale compared with first-hand environmental encounters. That we learn from novelists like Proust and Bellow. Idiosyncratic experiences and individual differences are common. Moreover, different perfumes are preferred in different cultures (Byrne-Quinn 1988), just like foods.

Observation of newborn infants is instructive. In one study (see Engen 1988) fifteen newborn babies—seven boys and eight girls, two and three days old—were tested with popular perfumes, such as L'Air du Temps, Maximi, Jontue, and Cachet. The perfumes were presented to the babies on a cotton swab. The effects were measured as changes in respiration, heart rate, and general activity. The babies responded to the perfumes, but there was no evidence that they preferred one perfume over another or, indeed, perfumes over other odors.

The first odor preferred by an infant is most likely that of its mother, whether a perfume or a natural body odor (Schleidt and Genzel 1990). Immediately after birth, an infant is just as likely to turn toward the odor on a cotton pad as toward that of its own mother. However, with time and increasing experience with its mother, turning toward her odor becomes more and more likely (MacFarlane 1975). The same learning principle applies to adults. In a large international survey of dispositions toward various odors, it was found that the body odors of spouses, friends, and children were generally described as smelling good (Schleidt, Neumann, and Morishita 1988). But the same kinds of odor were judged unpleasant in general and especially unpleasant in strangers.

After the death of his wife, Gracie Allen, George Burns found that sleeping in her bed was comforting. Such feelings are probably mutual for happily married couples. Although most people may dislike the odor of cigars, to Gracie Allen it must have been pleasantly associated with her cigar-smoking husband. Schleidt and Hold (1982) tell a story about a boy who was sad because his mother was in the hospital. At home he found one of his mother's shirts, which he pressed against his face like a security blanket. This kind of emotional uplift from a specific odor and its associated attachment is usually noted in children, but of course it is not limited to them. In adults it is more likely to be revealed under emotional strain. A mother of one of the young women murdered by the serial killer Ted Bundy sought comfort from the scent remaining in her daughter's personal things.

The search for perfume molecules and receptors by osmotherapists assumes that the perception of odor is analogous to the perception of color, which is elicited when different wavelengths of light affect certain photoreceptors in the retina. Such a stimulus-response mechanism explains the perception of quality, but not the acquisition of individual color preferences. Similarly, while there is a peripheral mechanism in the olfactory epithelium for discriminating odor qualities, it does not determine odor preference. Preferences are acquired either through conditioning or adoption of the common attitudes of people in a given culture. Perfumes do not sell themselves; their popularity must be understood in terms of associative learning theory applied to individual life experiences.

7

Body Odors

Body odors pose special problems. As noted in Chapter 5, they are a major indoor air pollutant, but they are also assumed to play an important role in kinship recognition and selection of a mate. Presumable odor strength is important. When strong enough to be noticeable, body odors are repulsive and motivate avoidance, but at lower concentrations they are said to be attractive aphrodisiacs. The latter possibility is a main topic of this chapter.

In animals, chemical communication between individuals is described under the heading of pheromones (Keverne 1987). Hormones are emitted into the air by one individual and are received by another at either one of two sites, the olfactory or the vomeronasal organ. The latter is a structure located in the septum that may be specialized to respond to pheromones (Wysocki 1979). Since this chemosensory system is vestigal in humans, any human pheromones must be mediated by the human sense of smell.

Several odor pheromones involving fear and aggression, the marking of territory, and choice of nutrients as well as sexual behavior have been indicated for animals. One is a primer, which elicits change in the olfactory receptor physiology due to odor stimulation. Another is a releaser, causing an immediate change in behavior when sensed. A third kind of pheromone involves olfactory imprinting, by which timing of the exposure to an odor during a critical period of development may affect later adult sexual behavior. Another is an informer, which draws out information stored in memory and thus influences choices of action (see Müller-Schwarze 1977). Other kinds of pheromones may be more relevant to the human situation. Although the evidence is not clear, there may be such "chemical messengers" playing a role in kinship recognition and interpersonal sexual relationships.

KINSHIP RECOGNITION

It has been proposed that odor stimulation provides an important basis for discriminating between one's own kin and others, between the "self and the nonself" (Thomas 1974). Odor may thus control symbiotic relationships and encourage outbreeding. Animal research shows that inbred mice can discriminate the odor of urine of close relatives from that of strangers, a capability that involves the histocompatibility complex (see Goldstein and Cagan 1981).

A person's body odor will be affected by environmental factors. Eating garlic is but one familiar example. Stress is another. However, each individual may have a unique odor, an "odor print," analogous to a fingerprint, and this is presumably the reason that dogs can be trained to track the odors of people. The olfactory systems of dogs are more sensitive than physical equipment such as gas chromatographs and flame-ionization detectors, but it is interesting to note that even bloodhounds have difficulty discriminating between identical twins (see Sommerville and Gee 1987).

Humans also show evidence of being able to detect differences in body odor. Blindfolded mothers can recognize the undershirts of their own infants based on odors. And children are apparently able to discriminate their own odor from that of others: One study showed that at the age of two or three, children were able to identify their own T-shirts among those of their playmates (Schaal 1988a). These data average performance to be better than chance but still error-ridden and far from the capability of bloodhounds.

It has been speculated that the olfactory system functions like the immunological system. Experience with chemical agents in the environment and memory of their molecules is important for both systems. Because of immunological memory, the nervous system remembers the response to vaccination (Salk 1987), and this might be analogous to the memory of odor associated with significant events and people. The activities of both systems could be the result of modification of the receptor functions caused by exposure to environmental agents. There are as yet no hard data demonstrating such changes in the olfactory receptor system, but such a priming effect is possible in the human sense of smell.

SYNCHRONIZATION OF MENSTRUAL CYCLES

The menstrual cycle of women who regularly live together in large families or in dormitories tend to be in synchrony (McClintock 1971). There are experimental reports that rubbing underarm gauze pads worn by women on the upper lip of another woman will cause the cycle of the second woman to synchronize with that of the first (Russell, Switz, and Thompson 1980). Such experiments must extend over months and are difficult to perform scientifically (Filsinger and Fabes 1985), but there is ample evidence for the so-called McClintock effect, as the following data collected by one of my students at Brown University show (Triedman 1981).

Forty-six students—twenty-three pairs of roommates all close to nineteen years of age—participated in the experiment. They were given a general description of the purpose of the experiment but were not given any information about the hypothesis of

synchrony. The students were in good health and did not use any
medications or birth-control pills. Beginning soon after they had
moved in together and every month for the next four months, the
onset of their menstrual periods was recorded. The main finding
was that the onsets of the periods of roommates took place more
and more closely throughout the semester.

The mean difference in the onsets at the beginning of the
semester was 19.6 days. The difference reduced to 17, 12, and 7
days after one, two, and three months, respectively. Even greater
synchrony would be expected after longer durations, but after
three months there was a one-month break for Christmas vacation.
When the students returned after one month, the difference was
back up to 12.9 days. In addition to the average time spent with
roommates, the company of male friends and other factors can
also affect the results (McClintock 1971).

No specific odor has been identified, but the process of eli-
mination of other explanations leaves the hypothesis that this
effect on the menstrual cycle is mediated by olfaction. It is also
not known what the purpose of the synchrony might be, but
an anthropological hypothesis proposes that it prevents a single
woman from being the only fertile one in a group and therefore
the only one attractive to strange males (Stoddart 1988). This
is not relevant in contemporary society, but it was important
for our primitive ancestors. While the men were away hunting,
the women were left together in the camp, and uniformity would
then help protect them. In addition, synchronization of a woman's
cycle with the whole group would help keep her faithful when her
husband was absent by reducing the chance that she alone would
attract other males.

MENSTRUAL CYCLE AND ODOR SENSITIVITY

There is evidence that the sensitivity of women to odors varies
during the menstrual cycle and that they are more sensitive
during ovulation than during menstruation. A change occurs in
the concentration of an odor required for the olfactory system

to respond. It is a small and subtle effect, as is true for all the effects of body odors considered in this chapter.

To Attract Women

LeMagnen (1952), who proposed this hypothesis, believed that the change in sensitivity applied only to certain biologically and sexually significant body odors—in particular, musk. Using a synthetic musk called Exaltolide, he observed that odor sensitivity remains at about the same level through the period of approximately twenty-eight-days except for a decrease beginning with the onset of menses and an increase at the time of ovulation. Musk's odor is difficult to describe, but it is believed to be similar to the odor from sections of human apocrine sweat glands. Women presumably are attracted by this odor, especially during estrus. Sexual motivation is the popular explanation, but *"le phénomène de l'exaltolide"* has another simpler and less exciting explanation.

The change in sensitivity may only reflect the fact that the olfactory mucosa is different during menses and ovulation. Estrogen production and other factors unrelated to sex but associated with the cycle affect the likelihood that odorous molecules will reach the olfactory receptors (Mair, Bouffard, Engen, and Morton 1978). The receptors are immersed in mucus, which the odorous molecules must penetrate to reach them (Ebling 1977), and the extent to which the molecules are absorbed into the mucus depends on their physical properties. The molecules of musk are relatively large and have relatively high boiling points, and thus they are less likely to reach the receptors than are other molecules. These physical characteristics are also associated with a longer retention time in the gas chromatograph, which provides a model for the interaction between odors and the olfactory mucosa (Mozell and Jagodowicz 1973). Odors such as amyl acetate ("banana") that have molecules with lower boiling points have a shorter gas chromatographic retention time than musk, and according to the present psychophysical hypothesis they would be expected to show little if any difference in absorption during ovulation and menstruation.

To test the hypothesis, odors with different physical characteristics were compared during ovulation and menstruation. The prediction was that coumarin ("new-mown hay") and cinnamyl butyrate ("cinnamon"), which have physical properties like musk but are not known to have any of the "biological significance" LeMagnen ascribed to musk, would still be subject to the same cyclical change in sensitivity. On the other hand, it was predicted that amyl acetate ("banana"), also not "biologically significant," would not be subject to change during menses and ovulation. The results supported these predictions—that is, women were less sensitive to coumarin and cinnamyl butyrate during menstruation than during ovulation, just as they were to Exaltolide. But for amyl acetate there was no difference in sensitivity during these two times.

The threshold shift, then, depends on the physical attributes of an odor that interact with biological changes associated with the menstrual cycle. The dulling sensitivity to musk at menstruation is caused by swelling of the nasal membrane, which in turn affects the accessibility of the receptors. This process does not have any direct implications for the control of sexual behavior. Indeed, its biological purpose is not known.

To Attract Men

Not only male odors are involved in intercourse. A female odor obtained from vaginal secretions and called "copulin" has also been suggested to have pheromonal properties (Doty, Ford, Prety, and Huggins 1975), but again an alternative interpretation cannot be rejected. Jellinek (1954) proposed that during menstruation an unpleasant trimethylamine odor masks the female erogenic body odor and serves as a warning signal similar to odors in some infectious diseases and inflammations. In other words, rather than the female becoming less sensitive, it is the male who may be adversely affected by odor and become less attracted to the female during menses. This too, however, is only a speculation.

ODORS AS APHRODISIACS

The odors of the animal ingredients used as fixatives in perfumes—musk, castoreum, civet, and ambergris—may also serve
a sexual function because they are similar to human body odors
associated with sweat glands. The chemical similarity is less
clear. All of the substances have disagreeable odors at high
concentrations, but in low concentrations they are used in a
class of sophisticated perfumes described as "oriental." Major
sources of human odors, the apocrine sweat glands, are found in
"the sternal region, the anogenital region, the mammary areola,
the cheek region, the eyelid, the ear canal and regions of the
scalp," according to Doty (1981, p. 354). Sweat is also produced
by the eccrine glands, found in the armpits and over much of the
rest of the body. Some of the components of these secretions are
found in both sexes, but the apocrine glands are larger and more
numerous in males than in females.

Some of the secretions of the apocrine glands are steroids,
similar to components in the animal secretions believed to be
pheromonal. One is androstenone, which is assumed to have an
effect on women similar to the effect it has on sows (see Kirk-
Smith and Booth 1980), in whose saliva it is found (Mykytowycz
1977). If a sow is exposed to this steroid during estrous heat,
she will assume a mating position. No one has suggested that
adrostenone has such effect on women, but it may change their
mood and initiate sexual behavior in some more subtle way.

In the study usually cited in support of the human pheromone
hypothesis, an attempt was made to influence where women
would sit in a dentist's waiting room (Kirk-Smith and Booth
1980). The experimenters sprayed some of chairs with androstenone in an aerosol solution and assessed the likelihood that
women rather than men would choose those chairs. Although
the secondary literature leaves the impression that there were
meaningful results, no simple difference related to sprayed versus

nonsprayed chairs was actually observed. There was no direct evidence that the women were attracted to the sprayed seats (or that men were repulsed by them). Any differences could be derived only from a complex statistical analysis of the factors manipulated in the experiment. These included the concentration of androstenone and how crowded the room was with people. As it turned out, the effect on behavior was not proportional to concentration, but for some unexplainable reason the women appeared to prefer chairs with a strong or weak concentration of androstenone over chairs sprayed with an intermediate concentration.

Another experiment (Gustavson, Dawson, and Bonett, 1987) indicated that men avoided college dormitory bathroom stalls odorized with androstenol, a related substance, but that it did not affect women one way or the other. With these possible exceptions, the question of whether or not body odors act like pheromones with effects like those of releasers has not really been tested with humans. Most studies use only questionnaires involving the rating of personal characteristics, such as attractiveness of people, rather than observations of direct influence on behavior or actual choices of action. It has been argued that when a man wears androstenone as a perfume, for example, he will be rated more favorably than he would be without it. However, like those of the study just described, these data also suffer from the lack of ability to relate findings specifically to androstenone and to exclude other factors (Black and Biron 1982). For the same reason, the concept of pheromones remains cloudy even in studies of animal behavior (Beauchamp, Doty, Moulton, and Mugford 1976). There is therefore no real evidence that androstenone elicits a specific human sexual response (Filsinger, Braun, Monte, and Linder 1984).

Body odor is after all not a clearly defined odor stimulus. Bacteria affect the secretions of the glands, and their odors are also influenced by diet and other factors. There is, in fact, no agreement about the hedonic properties of the odor of androstenone—or even a verbal description of it. At high concentrations, where it is more likely to be identified as body odor, it would seem aversive. Whether it is erogenous rather than antierogenous in dilute form is doubtful. There is some evidence that women are especially sensitive to androstenone (Gower, Nixon, and Mallet 1988), but this must be considered in light of the fact that they are generally more perceptive, as we will see in Chapter 9. At lower concentrations, androstenone is described with many different adjectives by different observers, ranging from "urine-like" to "fruity" and "floral." There is no typical response, and no evidence that women like the odor, even when it is weak. Although some do describe it as a pleasant odor, they do not constitute a majority.

Because natural human odors are likely to be present in intimate interpersonal relations, they are also likely to be associated with sex and, usually, pleasant experiences. For some, perhaps the first sexual encounter was not pleasant, and consequently they probably find such odors aversive. And if they are clearly identified as body odors in other contexts, most will find them disagreeable. Jellinek (1954) points out that "A maximum aphrodisiac effect is obtained by a combination of faecal and sweaty odours partly because . . . the resulting complex odour has a greater similarity with the complex 'body-odor' than the odours of each of the separate components" (pp. 173–174).

THE EFFECT OF LOSS OF ODOR SENSITIVITY

Based on the belief that odors control sexual behavior, it has been proposed that loss of the sense of smell (anosmia) means loss of the sex drive. There are indeed diseases involving both anosmia and a loss of sex drive. Patients with Kallmann's syndrome show both retarded genital development and anosmia. The cause is a hormonal deficiency, which is alleviated by administration of long-acting testosterone. Moreover, there is apparently a close connection between the sense of smell and the endocrine system (see Engen 1982). However, the question is whether or not the sex drive is reduced when only the sense of smell is impaired and all other systems remain intact. The answer is that it is unlikely, and a more realistic hypothesis, which has been considered by a number of psychiatrists (including Freud), is that the sexual drive may be attenuated with the loss of odor perception because normal functions may be enhanced by normal sensory input.

Odor preferences are established during life's pleasant and unpleasant experiences and become intimate parts of those experienced, whether they involve body odors, fragrances, or food flavors. The effect is in principle the same for all three. However, while the loss of odor perception practically destroys the ability to perceive food flavors, its effect on sex is minimal. Moreover, compared with someone who has acquired anosmia through disease or trauma, a person with congenital anosmia who has had different experiences from the beginning perceives food quite differently and can enjoy it without the odor component (see also Chapter 9).

MOTHER-INFANT BONDING

Whether body odors attract or repel depends on the associations a person has previously made to them, and such association may involve sex as well as factors unrelated to it. The odor of androstenone may be liked because of the positive nonsexual experiences women might have had with perfumes that have a similar odor. And it might also be a preferred odor because of positive experiences with men and their odors.

The establishment of such associations is similar to imprinting, but it is not restricted to a certain age or sensitive period of development, as is imprinting. There is, however, extensive evidence of early odor learning in the animal literature. For example, attachment by the rat pup to its dam's nipple was originally believed to be caused by the pheromonal effect of the dam's natural odor. However, research has shown that a special natural odor is not required (Alberts 1981; Pedersen and Blass 1982). One can substitute the odor of an orange or any other odor for the dam's natural body odor. It is quite conceivable that a human baby can have experiences similar to those of the experimental rats and can form an attachment to either its mother's own odor or her perfume. The important function of bonding requires odor recognition, and recognition memory is a special talent of this modality.

I noted in Chapter 6 that infants learn to distinguish their mother's odor from that of another mother (MacFarlane 1975), and mothers also learn the odors of their infants (Porter, Cernoch, and McLaughlin 1983). A two-day-old baby shows no odor preferences, but in time and with experience preferences develop and the baby will turn more and more toward the mother's odor rather than that of a stranger. The motivational effect of the odor increases with age and experience, and at about age three it is an intimate part of the recognition of and attachment to mother (Schaal 1988a).

Infants twelve to eighteen days old have also been reported to learn about odors other than the one associated with the breasts and milk. They will orient toward their mothers' axillary odors, which have a special calming effect. Infants also learn to orient toward breasts perfumed with rose oil (Schleidt and Genzel 1990). Breast-fed babies show stronger responses than bottle-fed babies, presumably because their noses are directly on their mothers' skin. Mothers are also recognized better than fathers (Cernoch and Porter 1985).

The literature on responses to mother's milk is of longstanding interest among neonatologists. The evidence suggests that at about four or five days of age the babies are able to recognize mother's milk by its odor and can discriminate it from milk from a nurse or cow's milk (Schaal 1988b). The conclusion seems justified that at birth body odor has no pheromonal effect but that associations are learned so early and so quickly that they appear to be innate.

8

Odor Memory

Whenever I smell new-mown hay, as I noted in Chapter 1, the memory of my grandfather's farm automatically comes to mind. It was the first experience of a city boy on a farm during the haying season, walking through a field of clover behind a mowing machine pulled by a homemade tractor driven by my grandfather. A prototypical odor memory thus originates with a novel experience (though not necessarily a novel odor) and lasts for a lifetime. We all have such individual odor memories that stand out because of the timeless and vivid way in which they bring back the totality of an experience.

Like visual and auditory memory, odor memory is influenced by a number of factors: familiarity, similarity, and compatibility of stimuli and responses; age; effects of memory aids; and other psychological factors, including Freudian repression. Yet despite this, folklore has it that odor memory is better than memory in any other mode. This chapter proposes another theory.

Odor memory is distinctive simply because each modality serves a special function of responding to certain physical stimuli—but in addition to that, odor memory has special attributes. In some respects it is poorer than auditory or visual memory and especially in terms of the techniques that can be used to retrieve these items.

LIMITATIONS OF ODOR MEMORY

The excellence of odor memory is not based on its capacity for storing information. The number of odors stored in the memory of an average person is not known, but visual and auditory capacities are probably much greater. There is a myth that people can remember and identify thousands of odors. They can indeed discriminate between countless numbers of odor qualities when compared side by side, but their ability to identify precisely odors that are presented singly is actually unremarkable. Very little useful information can be obtained about an unknown odor in a room by simply asking human observers to identify it. The accuracy of such judgments is poor.

We tested this ability by first presenting subjects with arrays of odors to be identified separately (Engen and Pfaffmann 1960). They were given as much time as they wanted to check each odor and to compare it with the others in order to prevent any confusion of similar odors and to attend specially to odors that seemed unfamiliar. When a subject was satisfied that he could identify each of the odors, the array was removed and each odor was presented individually in a random order to test his ability to identify it with the opportunity for comparison removed.

The results showed that the number of different and qualitatively diverse odors one can keep separate and identify one at a time without confusing one odor quality with another was not in the thousands but only about sixteen—no better than one finds for other modalities, for example, for pure tones varying in pitch and loudness (Garner and Hake 1951). The larger the number of odors in an array, the more likely it is that even familiar odors such as licorice and vanilla will be confused. Better performance can be obtained by practicing with selected sets of

odors (Desor and Beauchamp 1974), but not enough to approach
the level suggested by the folklore. There is no evidence that odor
identification can be improved by grouping odors into categories,
as one can improve memory of letters and words by putting the
letters into words or the words into sentences.

Le Norcy (1988) provides an illustration of the limited ability
to identify perfumes. Her company was interested in the effect of
packaging on sales, so it conducted a test in which observers were
asked to compare the same well-known perfume presented in
three different bottles, the original and two distinctly different and
unmarked bottles. "The results of the experiment were striking.
Not one of the forty people tested realized that all three bottles
contained the same perfume" (p. 223).

Odor recognition is also largely influenced by stimulus gene-
ralization—that is, people are prone to incorrectly identifying
similar odors as the target. A large company with a best-selling
brand of fruit-flavored drinks by mistake one time labeled the
strawberry drinks as raspberry and vice versa. Thousands of
cartons had been sold before the mistake was discovered, and the
company expected to receive many complaints from consumers.
In fact, there were very few complaints and little evidence that
the discrepancy had been detected. Although these flavors are
different when compared side by side, they are easily confused
when encountered singly. Once a mental concept has been established—for example, by the label on the fruit-drink container—
perception will then agree with the label (Engen 1987). Likewise,
an Italian experiment showed that when strawberry and apple
odors were labeled as banana and apricot, respectively, they
were remembered in that way because extraneous cues apparently
dominate in describing an odor sensation (Batic and Gabassi
1987).

A related problem is that the sense of smell has limited access
to what is stored in its memory. The first dictionary definition of
memory is the ability to recall physically absent items—a date,
a tune, a face—but this is not possible with the sense of smell. I
cannot bring into my consciousness the odor of new-mown hay

as I can all the other aspects of the farm episode. A physically present odor is required to activate this memory system, and I must quote Nabokov (1970) again: "Memory can restore to life everything except smells, although nothing revives the past so completely as a smell that was once associated with it."

One does also, of course, recall memories of experiences with odors, as in the following story about two native New Yorkers in their mid-sixties sharing memories at a local watering hole (Bridges 1990). The Manhattanite told the Brooklynite:

What I remember most vividly is the aroma of toast at the old drugstore lunch counter. It was like no other. I don't know why; we toasted the same white bread at home, but it never smelled as good or as intensely as it did in the drugstores. Maybe it was the high-volume buildup that did it. I loved that aroma. It made me feel good just to inhale it. Sometimes today, I'll walk blocks out of my way to shop for something I don't need at Kaufman's on Lexington Avenue—the only pharmacy I know of that still maintains a real lunch counter—to drink in that toasty aroma. (p. 56)

Perfumers are said to be able to imagine how a perfume will change as ingredients are added to a blend, but do they have a nonverbal mental image of it that they can call upon for this purpose? Reports of such experiences are by definition subjective and tend to entangle the contributions of odor with other sensory information. One can recall at will the color and shape of a lemon, and even the feeling and grimaces associated with biting into it and perceiving its sour taste, without the odor sensation being present mentally. When one is told to imagine squeezing a lemon, the visual imagery is clearer and more vivid if there is an odor of lemon present (Wolpin and Weinstein 1983), but that is actual odor stimulation and recognition. What is needed is evidence that merely thinking about squeezing a lemon makes one sense the odor of lemon, but this has not been demonstrated experimentally, and I think it cannot be.

A dramatic example that might seem to involve a genuine experience of an odor in the absence of actual stimulation is given by the painter Avigdor Arikha, who in an interview describes his reaction to seeing again a book of sketches he had made as a child in a concentration camp during the early part of World War II:

When I opened it I had to ask my wife to take it away. It wasn't the drawings themselves, it was that smell: you know—well, perhaps you don't—the horrible odor of corpses. The notebook reeked of it, or that's what I thought till Anne told me that it had no smell at all. The stench was in my mind. (Hofstadter 1987, p. 55)

Did he actually experience the odor of the concentration camp or, rather, the memory of a terrible situation associated with an odor?

THE SPECIAL ATTRIBUTES OF
ODOR MEMORY

No Forgetting

The most prominent feature of odor memory is its imperviousness to time. It is actually better to think of this ability in terms of not forgetting rather than remembering. Odor memory serves the primitive protection function of making sure that significant events involving food, people, or places are not forgotten. While visual and auditory memory usually decrease with time, often exponentially in light of new experiences, odor memory remains intact. In fact, odor perception tends to be conservative to the point of strongly resisting change in light of new information indicating that it ought to change. It is specialized for the ability to reinstate the past and to ignore subsequent odor experiences not associated with the formative event.

Even the memory of poorly learned odors remains unchanged. For example, in one experiment (Engen and Ross 1973) subjects were asked to memorize some fifty odors. Later, their memory was tested with a random sample of twenty-one of the odors, each paired with an odor that was not part of the original set. On the average the subjects could identify only about thirteen

(70 percent) of the previously memorized odors. However, they performed as well after one year as when tested shortly afterward on the same day. The lapse of time was not a factor. Some have speculated that perhaps the performance could not change very much because it was so poor to begin with. This is not the case. Performance will be more accurate in tests with fewer odors, but it remains unaffected by the lapse of time following the first exposure (Rabin and Cain 1984). For personally relevant odors, such as new-mown hay for me, the accuracy is nearly perfect (100 percent), both to begin with and forever.

Proust's famous recollections aroused by the aroma of a petite madeleine dipped in tea, which in a flash brought back long-forgotten events of his childhood, have been diagnosed as abnormal and labeled "Marcel Proust syndrome" (Douek 1974, p. 109). They are not abnormal. My memory of the farm scene, I believe, is just as vivid as Proust's of his youth in Combray. Most people report such odor memories, but needless to say, few describe them as well as Proust did.

Proactive Protection

Part of the timelessness of odor memory is that, unlike memory in other modalities, it is immune to the usual sources of interference with the learned connections between items. An odor association is a rigid bond not likely to be broken once established. A general psychological theory describes two main situations in which something can come between two associated items, disrupt their bond, and cause forgetting. When a target stimulus is presented and the subject remembers the last association, retroactive interference is said to diminish the first association. Experience of more recent associations decreases the ability to retrieve earlier ones. What has been learned recently tends to dominate in visual and auditory perception.

But the situation is different with odor memory. For this modality, proactive interference is characteristic. That is, the first association with an odor persists and dominates so that later associations with it can hardly be learned. We have demonstrated this kind of interference in experiments in which subjects learned to associate common odors with postcard pictures from different countries (Lawless and Engen 1977). The subjects were first asked to associate each picture with a certain odor—for example, the odor of cloves with a Scandinavian landscape. At the next learning session, the same odor was paired with a different picture: The odor of cloves was now paired with a landscape of Turkey. Later tests showed that the subjects remembered the first association, the Scandinavian scene, better than the second one, the Turkish scene.

Real-life incidents substantiate this laboratory observation of proactive interference, by which it is difficult to forget an odor association and to learn a new one, even when that would be the rational thing to do. Aversion is a common experience and a case in point (Logue, Ophir, and Strauss 1981). If strawberry has become associated with the dentist and pain because that is the flavor of his fluoridated water, not only will it be very difficult to get rid of this negative association, but it will even generalize to other situations involving strawberry. Unfortunately, it is not enough to understand how the problem came about in order to enjoy strawberry ice cream as something harmless, tasty, and even nutritious.

The association with the dental scene will render everything with that odor aversive. That may not seem rational, but it is prudent. One ought not to forget the events associated with pain. Such overgeneralized association has been observed in feral coyotes and wolves: After being made sick by contaminated sheep meat, they are strangely submissive when confronted with sheep (Gustavson, Kelly, Sweeney, and Garcia 1976). As Saul Bellow (1989) evocatively puts it, "Memory is life and forgetting death" (p. 72).

Why this cautious approach to odor? As I suggested in Chapter 2, the reason is that olfaction is a primitive survival system serving the function of quickly categorizing experiences with the chemistry of the environment without reasoning about them.

What one ought and ought not to eat must be learned quickly and unequivocally. The memory of the consequences must be protected, and that is the role of proactive interference. Environmental signals must be detected whenever they occur; to miss one could have unhealthy consequences, and when in doubt the system errs by sounding false alarms.

Encoding

Research on memory has traditionally focused on verbal encoding and the idea that in order to be committed to memory for later retrieval, an item must be named or labeled. As I have shown, odor memory in the laboratory is poor, even initially, before any time has elapsed during which forgetting might take place. The reason for this poor performance is not that the task is too demanding cognitively, for it only requires simple recognition without having to produce a specific name or label. Furthermore, the tests are usually taken by intellectually motivated students who are skilled at memorizing.

Requiring that odors be identified by name has been popular in both the clinic and the laboratory because it is akin to the use of the sense of smell in the real world. However, it is in fact difficult to judge single odors, to identify them absolutely when they are out of context. An average person with a normal sense of smell can only identify about 50 percent of common odors (Engen 1987).

Some have assumed that poor performance in certain odor-memory experiments (e.g., Engen and Ross 1973) results from the fact that (1) the situation is artificial and (2) many of the odors are unfamiliar and therefore are not named as well as odors experienced in the real world. I disagree with this view and propose instead that the problem involves the semantics of odors.

The odor-naming problem has traditionally been approached from the point of view of the chemistry of the odor stimulus. The theory has been that similar chemicals will elicit similar odor experiences and that these can be described by the same names. But research has failed to show any such intimate connection between odors and names. An odor does not elicit a universal name, as colors typically do. A different semantic system is involved.

Odors are named by function, what one does with them and in what context. Children generally follow this procedure in naming objects. Unlike adults, they do not use superordination in definitions. For example, children define an orange as something to eat. It is not until they are about seven or eight years old that more abstract ways of describing category membership, such as "an orange is a fruit," become evident in their language (Benelli, Arcuri, and Marchesini 1988). But we continue to name odors according to their functions as adults, when our descriptions of sights and sounds have changed.

At times one cannot come up with a word for an odor at all, even though one knows what the odor is (e.g., Hvastja and Zanuttini 1987). We have referred to this as the "tip-of-the-nose" state (Lawless and Engen 1977). A person will find himself in this state on an average of once for a series of ten common odors. He may be able to describe the unnameable odor as "medicinal" or to give some other general association, but he cannot be more precise, and he is always genuinely surprised when told what the familiar odor is. It seems obvious then what the name of the odor is.

There is other evidence of the tenuous connection between odors and their names and the role of names in retrieving memories of odors. Novel and unfamiliar odors may be described vaguely but are still in fact remembered accurately. In the recognition experiment already described that required a choice between old and new odors, an odor described vaguely as "strange" during the inspection part of the experiment would be recognized later on the memory tests as "that strange odor again" (Engen and Ross 1973). Other means of encoding than language must be involved. In general, the language used to describe odors is both impoverished and idiosyncratic (Engen 1982).

Although it is not crucial to odor memory, the name by which a subject is asked to describe an odor can affect subsequent performance in the recognition task (Cain 1979). On the average, it has been argued, the more specific the names the subject is provided for retrieval of odor memories, the better. In the literature this is described as "depth of semantic processing" (Craik and Lockhart 1972). For example, an odor described more veridically as "chocolate" is more likely to be recognized than one described as "candy," and "Johnson's Baby Powder" should be remembered better than "baby lotion."

However, although odors can be described very specifically, they are not, as I have noted, usually described at different levels of depth or in terms of a semantic system of super- and subordinates in the way that colors may be described in a hierarchical semantic system as red and pink. Although odor hierarchies may exist—for example, fruity–citrus–orange—one is hard put to find evidence that they are actually used. An analysis of the errors that are made is instructive. The odor of an orange is not typically described as "fruity" or "citrus" but as "orange." When another term is used, it will be another fruit or object that shares some characteristics with the orange. Thus, one will confuse mint with licorice and coconut with vanilla.

Experiments with the use of different odor labels (Engen 1987) suggest to me that what is described as lexical collocation (Halliday and Hasan 1976) is a better semantic model for how odors are encoded. Odors tend to be named with reference to certain contexts in which they occur or are used and with associates at the same level of abstraction. For example, the smell of onion may cause one to think of spices or pizza rather than plants and vegetables.

THE ROLE OF ODOR IN ENCODING
MEMORIES

Odor perception is situational, contextual, and ecological. Odors are not stored in memory as unique entities. Rather, they are always interrelated with other sensory perceptions—

gustatory, cutaneous, visual, auditory, and thermal—that happen to coincide with them. Unlike sensations of sounds and colors, odors can hardly be isolated and identified by their own names.

Odor perception is part of a larger context; it is ecological. All the various sensory aspects of this context are coordinated in a part of the brain associated with the hippocampus and amygdala, which is anatomically close to the olfactory input. The special contribution of odor sensation is its connection with this system and its ability to elicit the memory of an episode.

This is so despite the fact that one is not even necessarily conscious of odor at the time the associations are formed. The smell of hay was not in my conscious mind while I was walking behind grandfather's mowing machine. I was aware of the scenery, the tractor and its special sound, and the feeling of the cool, crisp air of a summer morning.

An odor is only an attribute of something else: an object, another person, an event, a certain environment. To the extent that these things are distinctive, their odors are distinctive. The odors are henceforth recognized because of their associations with things. Besides its ability to arouse attention, then, the sense of smell recalls whole episodes—both pleasures and pains—through such associations. This special ability is unaffected by the lapse of time and characterizes odor memory.

9

Loss of Odor Sensitivity

As is the case with all other human characteristics, there are individual differences in odor perception. Some people seem supersensitive to odors, and some have no sense of smell at all. In this chapter we examine people who have lost their sense of smell and their reactions to the loss. There is no literature on people with an excellent sense of smell; most of the data come from clinical studies in which patients are compared with other people with an average sense of smell. In order to understand odor deficits thoroughly, we must consider the statistics of individual differences in some detail.

Odor perception is generally automatic, so its value may go unnoticed. Only those who have lost the ability to smell know how to appreciate it, but even they may not think it critical and often hesitate to consult a physician about their condition. One patient who was totally anosmic ("smell-blind") after an upper respiratory infection decided that it was a cross she had to bear. Although she loved to cook, and she now no longer could enjoy doing it, she felt that other people had more difficult things to deal with. However, after an incident in which a toaster caught fire and she could not smell the smoke, she realized that she had lost a potentially lifesaving ability.

Another patient, a minister who often was visited by parishioners at his house, was embarrassed to learn from friends that the house smelled awful and had done so for a long time. Another person's odor is a taboo topic, and the friends had agonized over the matter before they decided that they had to tell him. They found a head of broccoli lodged behind a drawer in the refrigerator, where it had been out of sight for several months. This story is amusing, but only because it involves a rotten vegetable rather than a toxic gas.

One woman who was completely anosmic was brought to the clinic by her husband because he was worried about her. He had just arrived home and found the house reeking from the odor of rotten chicken meat, which she was about to eat. This followed another episode of her eating a cheese sandwich that she realized was mildewed when it fell apart after she had eaten half of it and she could see the cheese.

Those who have lost the sense of smell can use smoke detectors and have someone taste unknown foods for them. But the supply of such sensors is quite limited when judged against the many potential environmental pollutants in modern society. The superiority of the sense of smell resides in its constancy, its automatic functioning, and most of all its versatility in being able to detect different chemicals.

The American Academy of Otolaryngology estimates that some 200,000 persons each year consult a physician because of some deficiency in the sense of smell. There might be many more afflicted, because only those with the most severe problems are likely to seek clinical help. Less severely afflicted people (hyposmic) are less likely to consult doctors, and a biased data base is the result (Goodspeed et al. 1986). There is little statistical or epidemiological information about different degrees of impairment in the general population and their practical consequences. Leaflets issued by the academy describe anosmia as a

3 percent disability, but it is not clear what that means. Anecdotal evidence, on the other hand, is relatively easy to come by.

THE PSYCHOLOGY OF ANOSMIA

What is it like to lose one's sense of smell? It may begin with the experience of a change in odor perception following a virus attack or a head injury. In the elderly there may be a gradual decrease in the ability to perceive odors, similar to presbyopia in vision, and the term *presbyosmia* has been proposed (Van Toller and Dodd 1987). One can suffer a serious loss without being aware of it. It has a low cognitive priority. Even a complete loss may not be discovered for some time. One is not always conscious of odors and their absence as one is in the case of sight and sound. In addition, although the sense of smell may be seriously impaired, the fever and general misery associated with a virus infection are of more immediate concern. Once these symptoms have decreased, one becomes cognizant of problems with odor perception.

Although testing of a newborn infant's sense of smell is to be recommended because failure to detect odors might indicate malfunction of the forebrain, chromosomal disease, or diabetes, such testing is not widely performed (Sarnat 1975). Assume that a child is anosmic. How would the parents know? Visual deficits would be obvious within months, hearing perhaps within a year or two, but whether a baby perceives odors or not could go undetected indefinitely (Engen 1986a). When would an otherwise healthy child become aware of the absence of odor perception? He would have to be old enough to understand discussions involving odors, but even that would not necessarily resolve the problem.

A college student describes what it was like to grow up without a sense of smell. Her anosmia was not discovered until she was a teenager; it seems in retrospect that she must have lost the sense of smell when as a three-year-old she fell on her head into a cement drainage ditch and damaged the nerves between the nose and the brain. She did not appreciate the loss until a certain episode in which she discovered that, unlike all her classmates who talked about the smell, she failed to detect a gas leak in a high-school chemistry laboratory.

There were other times when people had asked me to smell something when I could not, but I thought this was because I was often congested and suffered from allergies. When my mother told me to hold my nose when eating liver or taking cold medicine to make it "go down easier," I noticed no difference and figured it was just another one of those things adults tell children to get them to do what they want them to do. The concept of smell completely baffled me, but I kept reassuring myself that once I outgrew allergies, smell would suddenly permeate my life. It did not.

When I told my family that I had no sense of smell, they didn't believe me. I didn't see a specialist until the summer following my freshman year of college, after being prodded by a close friend to find out for sure if I really couldn't smell. The doctor noted that the upper portions of my nasal passageways were still swollen from my allergies. He applied a solution to reduce the swelling, but I still couldn't smell rubbing alcohol on a cotton swab. I took zinc for a month, but it didn't help.

I began to wish I could tell what other people and especially men smelled like. Like the girls in the movies, I wanted to be able to hold the sweatshirt of the boy I had a crush on up to my face, inhale, and be overcome with his essence. A friend of mine had told me that he's heard that 40% of sexual interaction is based on conscious and subconscious olfactory cues.

The loss of smells does more than cut off a source of information about the environment; it changes flavor perception and the way one generally deals with the chemical environment. Here the distinction between hereditary and postlingually acquired anosmia is important. The perception of food by anosmics is not just weaker; it is qualitatively different. Normally, food flavors depend largely on odor perception, but to the anosmic taste sensations play a much larger role, as auditory signals do to a blind person. Some congenital anosmics report that they tend to breathe through the mouth to explore the air and, for example, enjoy the sweet taste of the outdoors after a rain but find stale air in a smoking area distasteful. One anosmic nurse said that on the one hand, she had the advantage over her colleagues in situations such as changing diapers, but on the other hand, she would miss the diagnostic odor clues to bedsores.

A person who lost the sense of smell through injury or disease feels a loss that a congenitally anosmic person could not experience. Conversely, if a congenital anosmic were cured, how would he know? What would the experience be like? There is no odor memory to rely on. One might guess that he would have experiences similar to the visual experiences of patients who have had cataracts removed as adults, thereby making normal vision possible for the first time. At first they are capable of simple sensory tasks like reporting colors, and perception of even rudimentary visual patterns requires months to develop (Hebb 1958). The cured anosmic would respond like the newborn babies in our experiments who become aroused by odors but show no clear preferential or hedonic response to them.

Although they perceive the world differently, there is no reason to think that congenital anosmics enjoy life less than those with a normal sense of smell. Their experience is quite different from those who had a sense of smell and then lost it. There is no evidence that congenital anosmia negatively affects self-concept, interpersonal relations, or quality of life. Anosmia does not have the serious cognitive and emotional consequences that blindness and deafness have, but any loss of information that cannot be provided by other sensory modalities is of course a handicap. What seems quite clear is that anosmia, whatever the origin, puts a person at risk in exposure to odorous toxic substances.

THE UNITY OF PERCEPTION

The sense of smell does not exist in isolation but is intimately related to other modalities and is influenced by their inputs, including temperature and even motor activity in chewing food.

It is especially involved with the workings of the gustatory and trigeminal systems.

Taste

Besides its vital function in monitoring the air, the sense of smell plays an essential role in assessing food. Food is suspect if it does not smell right. Although food flavor is usually experienced and described as taste, its perception is primarily one of odor (Murphy, Cain, and Bartoshuk 1977). A large percentage—perhaps the majority—of people who consult an otolaryngologist, or ear-nose-and-throat physician, with complaints of having lost their ability to taste food actually have lost the sense of smell. There is a profound confusion in the perception of what is gustatory input (mediated by cranial nerves 7, 9, and 10) and what is olfactory (mediated by cranial nerve 1) even though they stimulate two anatomically and physiologically separate systems.

Irritation

One more source of confusion concerns which nerves may be responsible for another kink of sensation. In the nose are both olfactory and trigeminal receptors which are connected to cranial nerve 5 (Meredith 1987). Trigeminal receptors respond to potentially harmful chemicals, such as ammonia, which also stimulate the sense of smell. Whether or not trigeminal stimulation is annoying depends on its strength and on prior experience with the particular stimulus. At low or even moderate concentrations, trigeminal stimulation does not necessarily seem unpleasant, and in some cases it can even become part of an acquired flavor preference. Because of positive experiences with dishes containing pepper and causing mild irritation or something akin to it, trigeminal stimulation is to many people part of a desirable "hot" food flavor (Rozin and Schiller 1980). Like odor and taste, the modalities of odor and irritation are anatomically and physiologically different, but naive perception does not reveal the extent to which each system is activated by a given substance (Engen 1986b).

Laboratory experiments show some characteristic differences between these modalities. The free endings of the trigeminal nerve are located deeper in the nasal mucus than the cilia on which the olfactory receptors are located. The sense of smell is more sensitive and is activated at lower concentrations of a substance than is the trigeminal nerve. The sense of smell is also quicker to respond—that is, it has a shorter reaction time—than irritation. On the other hand, odor sensations are likely to be diminished because of adaptation, but irritation persists and even increases over time (Cometto-Muñiz and Cain 1984). Finally, irritation has a more direct effect on respiratory and cutaneous systems and is more likely to cause pathology. Alarie (1973) has presented a review of research showing that irritation provides a highly reliable index of the effect of airborne chemicals on respiration. By comparison, the sense of smell serves only as a warning system regarding the existence of such annoying chemicals and does not initiate any systematic protective, physiological function. Although a patient has lost the sense of smell, the trigeminal system remains, but as in the case of flavor, perceptions will be altered and unfamiliar.

DIAGNOSTIC TESTS

Because of the need for greater attention to olfactory impairment, several taste and smell clinics were established with federal government support during the 1980s. There are some standard tests used in these clinics. A taste test is included because taste and smell are intimately connected and, as we have seen, patients typically report they have lost their taste when in fact the problem is olfactory. On this test the patient is asked to identify the four so-called taste primaries of sweet, sour, salty, and bitter. A test with ammonia or some other trigeminal stimulus ensures that this system is functional.

There are two primary tests of odor perception. One assesses sensitivity with a threshold test that determines the minimum concentration of an odor that a person can detect. Another, less common, test of sensitivity measures a patient's ability to perceive and rate changes in concentrations of an odor, varying from just above threshold to a level where it is quite strong (see Moskowitz, Dravnieks, Cain, and Turk 1974).

The other primary test attempts to determine the most serious impairment of odor perception, which is a decrease in the ability to discriminate between different odor qualities. While the threshold and scaling tests probe only the ability to perceive odor strength, an odor identification test probes a patient's ability to recognize and identify common odors, such as lemon, bubble gum, and peanut butter.

It has been assumed—traditionally but incorrectly—that sensitivity to certain odors as measured by the threshold test of odor strength predicts the ability to perceive and discriminate between different odor qualities. The threshold test makes it possible to evaluate a patient's problem only quantitatively and to categorize the degree of their deficits as anosmia versus hyposmia. But the distinctions between these pathological conditions are arbitrary, and one category shades into the other. The problem is more serious for the pathological perversions of odor quality perception, such as cacosmia (unpleasant odors from sinus infections) and parosmia (distortion of odor quality perception), which are described in the medical literature (Douek 1974).

There is no firm psychophysical or physiological basis for any of these terms, and therefore no agreement among medical people about usage. The general assumption is that the human sense of smell is similar to color perception, which can be described in terms of primary colors. Specific photoreceptors are activated by visual stimuli formed from combinations of primary colors. There are no analogous facts about olfaction; the nature of the whole transduction mechanism is unknown. However, this is now a very active field of research. There are several factors—heredity, gender, and age—that affect odor perception. We will turn our attention to them now.

CAUSES OF INDIVIDUAL DIFFERENCES

Heredity

Some are born anosmic, others with a keen sense of smell, but more specific information about the effects of heredity and congenital versus environmental factors is not yet available. An anosmia might conceivably be either specific or general. For example, one person may seem unable to smell the sweaty odor of isobutyric acid, yet he may be sensitive to all other odorants. Another person may seem unable to smell the skunky odor of butyl mercaptan, but he may be sensitive to all other odors, including isobutyric acid. Each of these people presumably lacks a certain olfactory receptor (Amoore, Polosi, and Forrester 1977). This could analogous to blindness to certain colors: for example, a protanope who is insensitive to red. A competing hypothesis is this: Rather than each receptor being responsive only to a specific chemical, all olfactory receptors are generalists but respond in different patterns to different chemicals. These are merely speculations at the present time; more data are needed on representative groups of the population.

Gender

A gender difference has been observed by many researchers (e.g., Cain 1982; Doty 1986). The following experiment (Engen 1987) illustrates the differences in performance. Twenty-five women and twenty-three men of college age were asked to identify each of ten common odors: banana oil, Bazooka chewing gum, lemon, clove oil, Crayola crayons, Ivory soap, Johnson's baby powder, mint, rose, and Vicks Vaporub.

The results were that while the women on the average obtained a score of 4.9 correct of the maximum possible of 10, men scored 4.1. The difference is statistically significant but too small to be obvious in real life. (The fact that both groups performed so poorly is just as interesting; one finds it hard to believe until put to a test oneself without any visual or other cues than odor.) The hypothesis favored in the literature is that the difference reflects an innate biological difference related to the endocrine system (see the discussion in Chapter 7). Another possibility is that the difference has nothing to do with olfaction but only reflects a difference in verbal ability: Women, according to this view, seem better able to find the words but do not have a keener sense of smell.

A third possibility is of course that both the endocrine system and verbal ability may contribute to the difference in performance. Culture and biology interact. Broverman, Klaiber, Kobayashi, and Vogel (1968) review related data indicating that steroid sex hormones implicated in odor perception may also have cognitive consequences. One basic observation is that estrogen is activating and androgen inhibiting. Estrogen presumably makes it possible for women to perform better than men on relatively simple tasks, such as visual acuity and naming of colors and, perhaps, odors. Because of their larger androgen supply, men do better than women on other tasks not involved in tests of odor perception. One example is a test of choice reaction time, in which the subject must turn off a light with one of two switches, depending on the color of the light. The subject must resist "jumping the gun," flipping a switch before deciding what the color is and thus which switch is appropriate.

Hormonal differences are already established in utero, and they could apply to children as well as adults. (The hypothesis of human pheromones, which also involves hormonal differences, does not apply to children [Koelega and Köster 1974].) To find out whether girls do better than boys, we tested newborn human infants selected randomly from a larger sample in a hospital epidemiological study (Lipsitt, Engen, and Kaye 1963). We found no evidence that girls are more sensitive to odors than boys at this early age.

However, there is another indication of a difference between boys and girls regarding odor perception. Balogh and Porter (1986) tested the reactions of children who were a little older, one dozen girls and one dozen boys twelve to eighteen years old. The infants were first exposed to one odor—either ginger or cherry—in so-called familiarization trials. Then, in the subsequent test of memory, the now familiar odor was put on one side of each infant's crib and an unfamiliar odor on the other. The boys turned indiscriminately to either odor, but the girls on the average oriented for 75 seconds to the familiar (and therefore perhaps preferred) odor and only 20 seconds to the unfamiliar one.

Postlingual children age four and older have been tested for their ability to select the correct label presented among three foils on a four-alternative multiple-choice test that requires selecting a word with which to describe an odor (Doty 1983). They do not do as well as adults at this task. Their scores keep improving until they reach age twenty, but at any age girls do better than boys. At age ten, for example, girls score 90 percent correct versus 75 percent for boys. This does not show that girls perceive odors better than boys or remember odors more clearly, but rather that they are better at selecting names by which to describe odors.

The gender difference is evident throughout the life span. For example, at age seventy women select the correct name for about 75 percent of odors and men for about 66 percent. There are, as far as I know, no data on the effect of the change of hormones in old age. In one unpublished study I tested a healthy postmenopausal sixty-year-old woman through three cycles with a hormone treatment to simulate the menstrual cycle and to prevent osteoporosis. She was taking estrogen for twenty-five days, to which progesterone was added on day 16. She took no drug for five days beginning on day 25. A large number of tests through the three cycles showed no effect on odor sensitivity.

Age

There have been a number of studies indicating that aging affects odor perception for women as well as men (Murphy 1986; Van Toller, Dodd, and Billing 1985; Schemper, Voss, and Cain 1981; Schiffman 1979). After reaching a maximum at about age twenty on the test described above (Doty 1983), the scores remain stable with increasing age until about fifty, when they begin to fall off, reaching a chance level of 25 percent after age eighty. It is important to note, however, that there are also very large individual age-related differences. The scores on a simple recognition task are relatively stable, and individual differences are of small concern in the age range of twenty to fifty; but for those older than fifty, while the average scores decline, at the same time individual differences increase. Children also vary more than adults in the twenty-to-fifty age range. In other words, the younger the child and the older the adult, the less representative are the norms for age. A person's age is therefore not by itself an adequate predictor of that person's ability to match verbal labels to odors.

For age ten the average is a score of 31, but the scores cover a range of 20 points, from 20 to 40. For an adult between twenty and fifty, the average is about 36, with a range of only 6 points, from 34 to 40. At age seventy the average is 28, with a range from 10—a chance level on this four-alternative multiple-choice test—to 40. Some very old people perform as well as people younger than fifty. The increase in individual differences is remarkable, and it is just as important as the decline in the average score. Furthermore, it cautions us against imposing a simple statistical definition of abnormality.

It is generally accepted that the decline in odor perception is similar to that in hearing and vision and that it reflects a deterioration of the receptors. The data are not clear because, as

I have noted before, these receptors have not yet been identified (Engen 1977). In fact, there is evidence of regeneration of olfactory receptors, but whether that has any practical consequences relevant to aging is not known.

Medical Factors

The most common causes of the loss of the sense of smell are upper respiratory infections, viruses, allergies, and sinus problems. Another cause is accidental trauma with damage to the head, when the soft neural tissues are jolted within the rigid skull (Costanzo and Becker 1986). This can cause the olfactory nerves to be sheared off at the cribriform plate, the bony part of the skull where these neural connectors from the receptors enter the brain, and this probably means a permanent loss of odor perception, as in the case of the college student discussed previously. In less severe accidents some nerves could be sheared off, leaving a person partially anosmic. The trauma may not injure the nerves but may cause nasal swelling and edema, which can temporarily interfere with transmission through the nerves.

Loss of odor perception may be iatrogenic, caused as a side effect by medicine or surgery. One patient I tested had a good-looking nose but no sense of smell. Plastic surgery for cosmetic purposes had affected the nasal passages and interfered with the normal air flow to the olfactory receptors. Deleterious side effects from drugs such as streptomycin and morphine have been suggested, although no specific data seem to have been published.

One sixty-two-year-old man wrote that he had lost his sense of smell following surgery to remove a tumor from his pituitary gland. One approach to surgery on the pituitary gland does, in fact, use the nasal passages as a gateway. On the other hand, the condition of acromegaly may cause one to become hypersensitive. Not only is the pituitary gland close to the olfactory bulb, the primary neural center for transmission of olfactory information to the brain, but it is also connected to the hypothalamus and is involved in the communication between the neural and endocrine systems.

Overexposure to olfactory stimulation, as we saw in Chapter 3, may have adverse effects. The system is robust, but its tolerance may be exceeded in some kinds of work using certain chemical substances (Amoore 1986). The olfactory epithelium of frogs, when exposed only for a relatively short period (one hour) to common industrial solvents (styrene, tolvene, trichloroethylene, and xylene) at high concentrations (ca. 1,000 ppm), shows structural changes in the mucus characterized by increased secretions as well as decreased physiological function measured by standard electrophysiological techniques (Ottoson 1980).

AFFECTED OLFACTORY MECHANISMS

Airflow

The most common loss of odor perception is analogous to a conductive hearing loss. Because of problems in the external auditory canal and the middle ear, sound is not transmitted to the receptors in the inner ear. Similarly, odor molecules, which must be carried through the nostrils with inhaled air, can be blocked on the way and may not reach the olfactory receptors. Whereas the windpipe, or trachea, is wide and straight and free of mucus, the nasal passages are narrow, especially at the inlet by the so-called valve area, where the opening is only about 1 mm (Proctor 1983). A light touch on the side of the nose will demonstrate that. The nostrils are complicated structures, with folds, or conchae, that keep air from flowing smoothly through them. They are lined with mucus and densely packed cilia, which resist the airflow and thus serve to analyze and filter the air. One can only estimate how many of the molecules available at the tip of the nose make it all the way through the approximately 7-cm distance to the receptors at the olfactory cleft under the brain (De Vries and Stuiver 1961).

A demonstration of the importance of the physics of the airflow of odors for the sense of smell is illustrated by laryngectomized patients, who cannot breathe through the nose and who are therefore functionally anosmic. A bypass has been designed to make it possible for these patients to draw air through the nose and to perceive odors as well as irritants (Mozell, Schwarts, Leopold, Hornung, and Scheehe 1986).

Blockage of the nasal passages because of sinus disorders and polyps is another example of interference with normal air conduction. Irritating pollutants in the air can cause inflammation and damage to the nasal passages and the olfactory epithelium. They are normally cleared by blowing the nose or are disposed of through the esophagus, but this system may fail because of overexposure or allergic reactions (Mygind and Lowenstein 1982). The exact mechanisms are not known, but some odors and all irritants, such as dust, fumes, and gases, may cause such reactions.

Receptors

In order to activate the olfactory system, chemical molecules must reach the olfactory epithelium at the top of the nostrils in the olfactory cleft, where the receptors are located. The mucus has a certain chemical consistency that may cause it to interact with the odor. It thus provides a critical environment for the operation of the receptors. Lack of vitamin A, hormones, and various chemicals, including arachidonic acid metabolites associated with polyps, could be the cause of loss of odor perception (Jung, Juhn, Wang, and Stewart 1987).

The receptors transduce the effect of the chemical into a neural response and experience of odor. The first inclination is to think that an odor-perception deficit is a problem of reception, but we have no direct knowledge about the olfactory receptors yet. Specific genetic problems or damage to the cilia caused renal or other diseases and trauma must affect them, but ideas about how that occurs are only hypothetical. Evidence has recently been obtained from samples of olfactory epithelium in human patients (Moran, Jafek, Carger, Roweley, and Eller 1985) showing that these factors may cause a reduction in the number of cilia and odor receptors. But such evidence is scanty.

Neural Pathways

Finally, problems involving the pathways to the brain and the brain itself may cause odor dysfunction. Difficulty in discriminating between different odor qualities, such as wintergreen and cloves, has been related to lesions in the prefrontal cortex. Evidence of this has come from patients suffering from Korsakoff's syndrome, which results from alcoholism and malnutrition and generally involves anterograde and retrograde amnesia. Kallmann's syndrome, mentioned in Chapter 7, afflicts the olfactory bulb. In Alzheimer's disease, the hippocampus and amygdala seem to be directly affected, and the disease spreads from there to the temporal, parietal, and frontal lobes of the cortex (Talamo et al. 1989).

Parkinson's disease and Down's syndrome also seem to affect the sense of smell. However, it should be borne in mind that all this evidence is tentative and not yet obviously relevant to the individual differences observed in the clinic and the problems addressed in this chapter. It is difficult to isolate the source of a given problem. Health will affect performance on any test. Cognitive deficiencies, such as forgetting and not being able to choose words, are also associated with diseases and with aging generally. They too may confound the results on odor-perception tests. However, there is general agreement that lesions in the pathways of the primary olfactory cortex and its thalamo-cortical projections affect ability to discriminate between odors; but, it is interesting to note, such lesions do not affect odor sensitivity (Engen, Gilmore, and Mair in press). Research with patients is making an invaluable contribution to the understanding of the physiological and anatomical correlates of odor perception.

TREATMENTS

Because of the lack of information about the olfactory system, the availability of treatments is quite limited compared with the ability to describe odor deficits. The loss of the sense of smell because of trauma is likely to be permanent. Sheared-off nerves cannot be repaired. Regeneration of receptors is limited to cilia and sites in the olfactory epithelium. Only a small percentage of regenerating axons find their way from the cells on receptor surfaces to the olfactory bulb (Moran, Jafek, Carger, Roweley, and Eller 1985). However, for most patients there is reason to be more optimistic.

Zinc sulfate, which is a very commonly prescribed remedy, can have a dramatic effect in certain cases. It has also been implicated in stunted growth cognitive problems in learning, as well as in interference with sexual maturation. Vitamin A is required for the olfactory epithelium to function normally (Duncan and Briggs 1962), and it may play a role in olfaction similar to its role in vision by acting on the glands and mucus and by promoting the moisture necessary for the transduction of olfactory stimuli. (There is, however, no evidence that these substances improve one's odor acuity, as some apparently believe.)

Treatment is often possible for loss of odor perception due to blockage of the airflow. Removing polyps surgically can improve the sense of smell, and systemic steroids can be used to slow down the return of the polyps. This treatment has been successful in maintaining the sense of smell for some time (Jafek, Moran, Eller, Roweley, and Jafek 1987). Dramatic results have been obtained with a cortisone called prednisone. One patient was put on this anti-inflammatory steroid to treat her anosmia caused by a swelling of the olfactory epithelium. She described the experience of tasting food and smelling her husband in glowing terms: It was as though the world had changed "from black and white to technicolor." But the ecstatic feelings were short-lived, because prednisone has undesirable side effects. The full effects of this steroid need to be learned, so that it can be used without, for example, affecting the immune system. In general, present knowledge cannot provide smelling aids analogous to hearing aids.

Because olfaction has such a low priority in medicine and because so little is known about it, diagnostic methods and treatments range all the way from sophisticated studies of brain cells to abstract analysis of the psyche. A college instructor describes the frustrating experience of losing her sense of smell (Birnberg 1988). The cause was not known, and therapy was based on trial and error. The initial examination revealed nothing biologically wrong, and it was therefore suspected, as is too often the case, that the problem was psychosomatic. After that possibility was rejected, it was decided that the problem was allergy and infection. Describing the continuation of her ordeal, Birnberg writes,

I have had a CAT scan, blood tests, sinus cultures, allergy tests, allergy shots, long-term zinc therapy, weekly sinus irrigations, a biopsy, cortisone injections into my nose and four different types of sinus surgery. My case has been presented to hospital medical committees. . . . I have been through the medical mill. (p. 10)

After suffering through this trial-and-error process, a patient is likely to come to think that it is a "mental" problem after all. The loss has a distinct effect on one's sense of well-being and self-assurance among other people, which contributes to this worry. Not surprisingly, there *is* a psychiatric literature involving odor perception, but that pertains to patients with a normal sense of smell who hallucinate odors when there are none present. One person sent me a twenty-page letter telling how she thought someone was trying to kill her with a poisonous odor and asking me how to get rid of it. The anosmic patient has the quite different problem of not being able to smell odors that are present.

Considering that the problem is often a conductive one, analogous to a loss in hearing because of otitis media or otosclerosis (which does not involve the nervous system), it would be reassuring to know at least that much about one's loss of odor perception. An important therapeutic function of a clinic ought to be to provide as much objective information as possible to a patient about (1) the problems caused by the lack of odor perception and (2) precautions the patient needs to take to avoid the dangers encountered by the woman described at the beginning of this chapter.

Clinical cases illustrate some of the more common problems when odor perception is deficient. In addition, there is—especially for the elderly—a possible loss of appetite and enjoyment of food ("It's all tasteless mush"), which in turn could lead to an inadequate diet. There are also often interpersonal problems one is not likely to want to talk about. Social problems can be a side effect of body odors or odorous medications. One woman used a smelly ointment that was annoying to her office mates but that she herself could not smell.

To provide useful information to any person concerned about the practical effects of the loss of odor perception has been the main purpose of this chapter. But I also want to underscore the very important loss of odor memory and of the pleasure of odor sensations. One sees a lilac in the spring and remembers the enjoyment of the odor experience, but one cannot retrieve it.

10

The Odor Sensorium

There are two approaches to the study of the senses. One, classical sensory physiology and psychophysics, begins with an environmental stimulus and follows its course from the receptors in the periphery to higher centers in the brain. This approach proposes that all perception can be understood from an analysis of that sequence of events and its mediating structures. Research in olfaction and its application in food science, perfumery, and the clinic has been largely influenced by this approach, which stresses the study of stimuli and receptors. These are interesting phenomena but they provide only a partial description of the sense of smell and do not explain how the sense is used.

Even at the simplest perceptual level, an odor is not a singular, isolated sensory event but one intimately associated with other sensory stimulation, especially that from gustatory and trigeminal activation. Moreover, odors are experienced in a personal way, which tends to make them distinctive. If odors were to be classified—an endeavor history shows to be unrewarding—the categories of the system would have to include cooking odors, pollutants, perfumes, and the like, rather than simple elements of odor sensations.

The second approach to the study of the senses emphasizes the fact that information coming from the periphery is dealt with and controlled at higher levels in the nervous system. The first scientific study of the senses in psychology showed that the response to a physical stimulus is determined not only by the stimulus's characteristics and the receptors it activates but by the brain itself, which in turn is influenced by experience. The early experimenters called this whole system "the sensorium" (see Woodworth and Schlosberg, 1954, p. 429).

To some observers the two approaches appear to be in conflict, but I think that they supplement each other. This chapter describes the central effects on odor perception in terms of what I call the "odor sensorium": the characteristics of the hypothetical innate system for controlling the reception and interpretation of olfactory stimulation and the response to it. The original concept of the sensorium was of one general system describing all sense modalities, but I propose that the odor sensorium is a special system.

There are special physiological features of olfaction that distinguish it from the other sense modalities. Olfactory receptors are more directly connected to the brain than those of any other sense, being only one synapse away from the olfactory bulb. They also have the most direct access to the environment of any modality and are the only receptors located outside the blood barrier. Because of this direct exposure to the environment, they are vulnerable, and this might be related to another special feature, a continuous process of regeneration. The olfactory receptors are presumed to be located on cilia. The receptor neurons are produced continuously from stem cells located along the basal lamina of the receptor epithelium. These cells are believed to regenerate and form new connections with the brain throughout the life span (Gesteland 1986; Graziadei and Graziadei 1978).

A final special feature is the location of the olfactory bulb at the front of the brain, where odor sensations are interconnected through primitive cortical structures to neocortical association areas. with other sensory input (see Figures 10.1a and b). The associative learning that is characteristic of odor perception can be assumed to involve storage and interaction under the influence of the amygdala, while the hippocampus ties the memory to a context involving a unique time and place and other sensory stimulation (Eichenbaum and Cohen 1987; Gerbrandt 1987; Price 1987). There is, however, no clearly demarcated "smell brain."

The following is a loosely ordered list of the interrelated functional attributes of the olfactory sensorium. All of them have been discussed in earlier chapters; they are summarized here with some elaboration and examples. Odor perception is not unique, for it shares attributes with other modalities in various degrees, but the following seven items define its special functions.

NEOPHOBIA

The immediate effect of a novel odor is apprehension. The sense of smell is easily aroused, and this arousal is uncomfortable. The first response, which is described here as neophobia for lack of a better word, characterizes the primitive modus operandi of olfaction. Infants who have no experience with odors make the same response to anise and asafetida (Engen, Lipsitt, and Kaye 1963). All odors evoke only apprehensive arousal.

For the same reason, adults respond with caution to any unfamiliar odor, or to an odor that at first whiff seems to be unfamiliar, and the longer it remains unidentified, the more defensive the behavior. Olfaction shares this sensitivity with hearing, but perception of sound reflects cognition, whereas perception of odor involves emotion and motivation. Certain speech sounds may have inherent meaning, but odors are meaningless until they have been experienced in a context. The olfactory pleasures of flowers, foods, and perfumes are acquired hedonic experiences. (Bear in mind that I am describing odor sensations free of trigeminal, or irritating, components.)

Figure 10.1a
The Anatomy of the Olfactory System (cross-section)

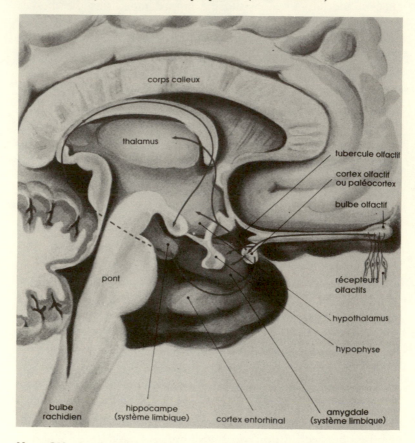

Note: Olfaction is often considered an old and primitive sensory system. Its primitive and simple organization is in particular illustrated by the fact that, unlike stimulation of other senses which follow a complex neural path, olfaction is a more direct one to the brain, as shown in Figure 10.1a.

Figure 10.1b
The Anatomy of the Olfactory System (from below)

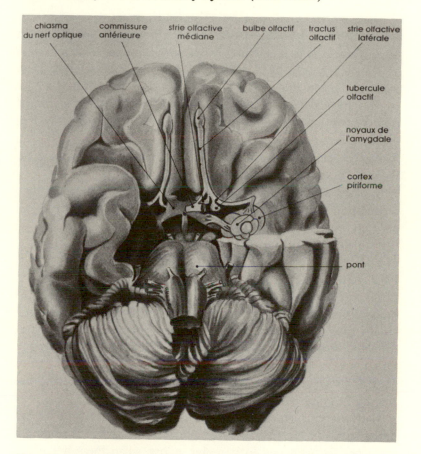

Note: Figure 10.1b shows further details of this system located at the base of the skull. Another characteristic of olfaction is its interconnections with the hippocampus and the amygdala of the limbic system which play important roles in perception and memory. These connections afford a strong connection between olfaction and the other senses, including audition and vision. They facilitate the formation and later retrieval of associations between odor and other events and their emotional context.

Source: Adopted from André Holley, *La Recherche*, 1989, vol. 20, pp. 172–173.

FALSE-ALARM RESPONSE BIAS

The sense of smell is a sensitive and inherently vigilant detection system operating under a strict decision rule: When in doubt, it assumes that there is an odor around. There is also a tendency to err by perceiving odors as strong rather than weak. A false-alarm rate of 5 percent would be high in a visual psychophysical experiment, but 20 percent is common in tests of odor perception—and it is often higher, as will be illustrated in the next few paragraphs. For this reason the tendency for false alarms to occur is what often turns out to be the most important factor in odor experiments.

In other words, the olfactory sensorium is set to overestimate stimulation and therefore is unlikely to miss the presence of an odor. It operates as though it is guided by what is called an "asymmetric payoff function" (Green and Swets 1974). The cost of missing an odor signal is more serious than that of raising a false alarm. This odor function is a bit like a soldier on the lookout for enemy warplanes, represented as blips on a radar screen. To prevent being attacked he must maximize the likelihood of hits, but in order that he not miss a single warplane, the criterion for what sort of blip he will use as evidence must be liberal. Of course, such a criterion also increases the likelihood of false alarms, but no real harm can come from that. The odor sensorium acts as though it were always at war.

The following experiment (Engen 1972) illustrates how expectation based on the frequency of actual odors in an environment increases the tendency to perceive odors when there are none. The subjects were asked to judge whether a cotton swab had an odor or not. There were 500 trials for each subject; in half of the trials there was a weak odor (n-butanol) on the swab, and the other half odorless diluent (water). Half of the swabs with odor and half of the blanks had been tinted pale yellow with an odorless dye. After practice with the various swabs, each subject received in a random order 125 of each of the following trials: clear blanks, tinted blanks, clear odors, and tinted odors. The subject received no feedback about his accuracy.

The percentage of false alarms reporting that the tinted diluent smelled was 70 percent (and thus only 30 percent correct responses that it was odorless). For the clear, odorless cotton swabs, the false-alarm rate was 51 percent—still very high, as is typical in odor perception. The percentage of hits—that is, correct affirmative responses—was a high 90 percent because of a general tendency to expect odor.

In real life one often does not obtain any information about the accuracy of one's odor-identification performance. Laboratory experiments show that being informed whether a response was right or wrong will improve performance and reduce errors. A follow-up experiment on the occasion I have been describing showed that performance was better with such feedback but that even when a false alarm would result in a loss of money paid to the subject it still was more likely to involve the tinted (22 percent) rather than the clear (14 percent) odorless cotton swab.

Yet another test with only clear swabs showed that increasing the frequency of occurrence of an odor will increase the likelihood of false alarms. In the previous experiments, blanks were presented in half of the trials and odors in the other half in a random order. For this experiment the percentages were changed. In one instance, there were only 50 swabs with odors (10 percent) in the 500 trials and the rest (450) were blanks. In a second instance, there were 450 (90 percent) odors and only 50 blanks (10 percent). The results show very clearly that hits increase with the frequency of odors (from 70 percent to over 91 percent). However, the percentage of false alarms increased even more (from 5 percent to 59 percent). It is clear that there is a strong inherent tendency to perceive odor.

PLASTICITY

Information about odors at normal strength is acquired quickly and perhaps typically after only one exposure. Aversion illustrates this, as do positive feelings about new fragrances or flavors associated with pleasant events. Plasticity also has another side, habituation. One quickly comes to ignore inconsequential odors. Even in the naive infant, cessation of the response to such odors takes place after but a few exposures. The many inconsequential odors in the environment become part of the ignored background.

The plasticity of the sense of smell is obvious in animals, and humans have taken advantage of it. Dogs can be trained to trace any specific odor, including completely unnatural signals, such as the smell of narcotic drugs, the body odor of a specific person, or the scent of termites, which could hardly have any natural significance for dogs. The dog has a large number of receptors available for these tasks, perhaps billions, an order of magnitude higher than the number of receptors in man. Humans have an estimated six million olfactory receptors in each nostril (Mozell 1987), which must be sufficient for learning whatever significant odor associations they may experience in a lifetime.

The classic Pavlovian paradigm has been thought to describe this learning, but it might better be thought of as a change in the response bias to an odor. One was aware of the odor before, but it has taken on a new meaning because of experience with it. This association to the event is formed only in retrospect, as though the odor were an incidental matter at the time the event was experienced. One becomes sick from eating a certain food, and afterward the odor of that food is aversive, a quality it did not have at the time it was consumed. Another example of the temporal characteristics of odor learning is this: It is not a perfume that makes a woman attractive; it is the other way around.

Odor likes and dislikes can also be learned in one's culture, without any direct experience. Thus, while our own bodily odors are perceived as neutral or even pleasant, we acquire the attitude that the body odors of other people signify dirt and disease. Another example is what happened to a newlywed couple on their honeymoon at a country inn. The bride came from a kosher home, the groom did not. In the morning, the smell of bacon wafting to their room from the kitchen below made her nauseous. To him, however, it had a pleasant association with breakfast time. Such associations persist in odor memory without any direct reinforcement.

ECOLOGICAL ENCODING

It is often observed that odors do not have their own names, as do sensations in other modalities, but that they are always described as smelling like other things. The traditional approach to odor perception described at the beginning of this chapter assumes that there is a certain stimulus causing an odor's particular quality. In vision, sensations can be understood in terms of basic stimulus attributes at the receptor level, related to and classified in terms of specific, unitary color names. To get around the problem that odors do not have their own names, but retaining the hypothesis that analogous stimulus-response relationships may be found, chemicals judged to have similar odors have been analyzed with sophisticated apparatus in hopes of revealing their significant stimulus techniques (Schiffman, Reynolds, and Young 1981). Such so-called similarity analysis has not been able to produce any general classes of odors. The reason, I would suggest, is that odors do not belong to classes determined by their chemical or physical attributes. They are coded in terms of sensations coinciding and interacting with them at higher centers in the nervous system. To a human being, the meaning of an odor is determined by its environmental associations, whether they be a person, an event, or an object. In that way the odor is, if not unique, at least special.

Flavor perception demonstrates how odors are intimately related to other experiences. Taste and odor components of a flavor are so integrated that they cannot be separated introspectively by the perceiver. Subjects in one psychophysical experiment judged mixtures of the sweet taste of saccharin and the fruity odor of ethyl butyrate at various concentrations (Murphy, Cain, and Bartoshuk 1977; Murphy and Cain 1980). The main finding was that odor was the dominant component affecting the perception of the mixture, but a change in odor was perceived as a change in taste. For example, adding a strong concentration of the odor to a weak concentration of the taste made the mixture taste five times stronger. By contrast, varying the amount of saccharin had no effect on odor perception. Similar experiments were performed with lemonade made of sugar and citral, in which the tasteless odor of citral affected the strength of the sugary taste.

The confusion of the sensations of taste and smell is a general phenomenon; it is not a semantic artifact, but a discrepancy between physical stimulation and perception, and a real illusion. That is the reason why losing the sense of smell is experienced as a loss of taste. The perception is under the control not of the stimulus but of the odor sensorium. There is central processing of the sensory information. An odor sensation is like a state that has no meaning by itself but obtains meaning from the situation in which it is experienced.

PROACTIVE INTERFERENCE

Odor preferences are like habits. They are easily established but difficult to change. The first association to an odor is protected by a mechanism called proactive interference (Underwood 1957). Once an odor association has been acquired, the contribution of the odor is to facilitate retrieval of the context in which it was experienced. The persistence of such associations in memory is the essence of odor perception. One reason that odors are not forgotten, as I have just observed, is that they are integrated into the mental representation of larger wholes; they have no names of their own but exist as parts of the larger wholes. That is why it is difficult to identify isolated odors in the laboratory or clinic. Odors do not have attributes like salty or red, by which they can be described and later identified.

Furthermore, because one odor does not share such attributes with other odors, it is also less likely to be confused with them. The simple but special role of odor perception is not analysis—reasoning why—but recognition of specific events. Having learned one association to an odor makes it difficult to learn another subsequently. That is why it is difficult to overcome aversions. Thus, an odor is a particularly unambiguous and unforgettable signal serving a primitive survival function.

RECOGNITION MEMORY

A salient characteristic of the sense of smell is its ability to remember—or rather, not to forget. However, contrary to popular thought, odor memory is not generally outstanding but is highly specialized. Evidence of memory is ordinarily obtained from both recall and recognition (Wingfield and Byrnes 1981); dictionaries usually emphasize the recall component. However, recall is not within the capacity of the odor sensorium; it is limited to recognition.

Odors are not recalled by words, images, or other items. Instead, they help recall experiences. When people talk about the odors they remember, they are referring to experiences and situations in which odor played an important part. They remember the seasons and the fact that spring brings fragrances with it. However, only the visual attributes are recalled; recreation of the fragrances is not itself part of the recollection. The odor sensorium does not have any retrieval ability; its main function is to respond to odors here and now and to deal with the consequences associated with them. In fulfilling that role it is unsurpassed.

While cognitive theories of memory developed for vision and hearing are germane to the extent that there are general cognitive attributes of odor perception, there are differences among the modalities that may be considered adaptive specializations. Research has illustrated this with genetic manipulation of fruitflies (Sherry and Schachter 1987). A fruitfly named Dunce is incapable of learning to avoid odors associated with electric shocks. A mutant, called Amnesiac, can learn the association but forgets it very quickly. I suggest that the odor sensorium acts like an idiot savant: It is very sensitive, learns quickly, and forgets nothing, but it has no judgment about what ought to be remembered and what might as well be forgotten. This modus operandi will lead to many mistakes and false alarms. However, it ensures the identification of odors vital to the individual's physical and psychological well-being.

AN EPIPHENOMENAL MNEMONIC

Odors only stimulate memory; they do not cause any other reactions by themselves. When one feels sick in the presence of an odor, it is not because of the odor itself but because of its association with previous sickness. Automobile exhaust smells and is deadly, but it is not deadly because it smells. The odor sensorium has no capacity for discriminating toxic from nontoxic substances. Odors are epiphenomenal, without any direct biological effect other than that on the olfactory system. Still, the powerful illusion that they cause pleasure and pain persists. Even when one knows that it was drinking too much whiskey that made one sick, the smell of it remains aversive as though it were the cause.

There are also no human pheromones or odor aphrodisiacs. An odor is only capable of conjuring up the memory of a sensual experience and does not directly motivate such behavior. Any odor that happened to be present on an occasion—the body odor of a partner, her perfume, the diesel odor of his car—may act like an aphrodisiac or a repellent, depending on the nature of the encounter.

What the nose knows, to use that popular expression, is to respond to chemical signals to keep us out of harm's way and to remind us of past odor experiences, both the foul and the fragrant.

References

Ahlstrom, R., Berglund, B., Berglund, U., Engen, T., & Lindvall, T. (1987). A comparison of odor perception in smokers, non-smokers and passive smokers. *American Journal of Otolaryngology, 8,* 1–6.

Ahlstrom, R., & Engen, T. (1987). *Discrimination between weak and strong odors by smokers, non-smokers and passive smokers* (Report No. 654). Stockholm: University of Stockholm, Department of Psychology.

Alarie, Y. (1973). Sensory irritation of the upper airways by airborne chemicals. *Toxicology and Allied Pharmacology, 24,* 279–297.

Alberts, J. R. (1981). Ontogeny of olfaction: Reciprocal roles of sensation and behavior in the development of perception. In R. N. Aslin, J. R. Alberts, and M. R. Petersen (Eds.), *Development of perception: Vol. 1. Audition, somatic perception, and the chemical senses* (pp. 322–357). New York: Academic Press.

Alin, L. H. (1986). Some facts and artifacts in psychological memory curves. *Göteborg Psychological Reports, 16,* 1–67.

Amoore, J. E. (1986). Effects of chemical exposure on olfaction in humans. In C. S. Barrow (Ed.), *Toxicology of the nasal passages* (pp. 159–190). Washington, D.C.: Hemisphere Publishing.

Amoore, J. E., Polosi, P., & Forrester, L. J. (1977). Specific anosmias to 5-(alpha)-androst-16-en-3-one and (w)-pentadecalactone: The urinous and musky primary odours. *Chemical Senses & Flavor, 2*, 401–425.

Balogh, R. D., & Porter, R. H. (1986). Olfactory preferences resulting from mere exposure in human neonates. *Infant Behavior and Development, 9*, 395–401.

Baron, R. A. (1988). Perfume as a tactic of impression management in social and organizational settings. In S. Van Toller & G. H. Dodd (Eds.), *Perfumery. The psychology and biology of fragrance* (pp. 91–104). London/New York: Chapman and Hall.

Batic, N., & Gabassi, P. G. (1987). Visual dominance in olfactory memory. *Perceptual and Motor Skills, 65*, 88–90.

Beauchamp, G. K., Doty, R. L., Moulton, D. G., & Mugford, R. A. (1976). The pheromone concept in mammalian communication: A critique. In R. L. Doty (Ed.), *Mammalian olfactory, reproductive processes and behavior* (pp. 143–160). New York: Academic Press.

Bedney, B. (1962). Mosquitoes. In F. D. Reeve (Ed.), *Great Soviet short stories* (pp. 37–71). New York: Dell.

Bell, P. A., Fisher, J. D., Baum, A., & Greene, T. E. (1990). *Environmental psychology* (3rd ed.). New York: Holt, Rinehart and Winston.

Bellow, S. (1989). *The Bellarosa connection.* New York: Penguin Books.

Benelli, B., Arcuri, L., & Marchesini, G. (1988). Cognitive and linguistic factors in the development of word definitions. *Journal of Child Language, 15*, 619–635.

Berglund, B., Berglund, U., & Lindvall, T. (1978). Olfactory self- and cross-adaptation: Effects of time of adaptation on odor intensity. *Sensory Processes, 2*, 191–197.

Berglund, B., Berglund, U., Engen, T., & Lindvall, T. (1971). The effect of adaptation on odor detection. *Perception and Psychophysics, 9*, 435–438.

Berglund, B., Berglund, U., & Lindvall, T. (1987). Models of sensory interaction. In A. Okada & O. Manninen (Eds.), *Recent advances in research on the combined effects of environmental factors* (pp. 283–294). Kanazazwa, Japan: Kyoei Co., Ltd.

Berglund, B. (1990). The role of sensory reactions as guides for nonindustrial indoor air quality. In D. M. Weeks and R. B. Gammage (Eds.) *The practitioner's approach to indoor air quality investigations* (pp. 113–130). Akron, Ohio: American Hygiene Association.

Berglund, B., Berglund, U., Lindvall, T., & Nicander-Bredberg, H. (1982). Olfactory and chemical characterization of indoor air: Towards a psychophysical model for air quality. *Environment International, 8*, 327–332.

Berglund, B., & Engen, T. A comparison of self- and cross-adaption to odorants presented singly or in mixtures. Unpublished manuscript. University of Stockholm.

Berglund, B., & Lindvall, T. (1986). Sensory reactions to "sick buildings." *Environment International, 12*, 147–159.

Birnberg, J. R. (1988, March 21). *Newsweek,* Living with a lack of taste, p. 10.

Black, S. L., & Biron, C. (1982). Androstenol as a human pheromone: No effect on perceived physical attractiveness. *Behavioral and Neural Biology, 34*, 326–331.

Bridges, H. (1990, September). Looking back. *Gourmet,* pp. 54–60.

Broverman, D. M., Klaiber, E. L., Kobayashi, Y., & Vogel, W. (1968). Roles of activation and inhibition in sex differences in cognitive abilities. *Psychological Review, 75*, 23–50.

Byrne, D., & Clore, G. L. (1970). A reinforcement model of evaluative responses. *Personality: An International Journal, 1*, 103–128.

Byrne-Quinn, J. (1988). Perfume, people, perceptions and products. In S. Van Toller & G. H. Dodd (Eds.), *Perfumery. The psychology and biology of fragrance* (pp. 205–216). London/New York: Chapman and Hall.

Cain, W. S. (1970). Odor intensity after self-adaptation and cross-adaptation. *Perception and Psychophysics, 7*, 271–275.

———. (1979). To know with the nose: Keys to odor identification. *Science, 203*, 467–470.

———. (1982). Odor identification by males and females: Predictions vs. performance. *Chemical Senses, 7*, 129–142.

Cain, W. S., & Drexler, M. (1974). Scope and evaluation of odor counteraction. *Annals of the New York Academy of Sciences, 237*, 427–439.

Caprio, J., Dudek, J., & Robinson, J. J., II. (1987). Prediction of olfactory responses to stimulus mixtures by cross-adaptation experiments. *Annals of the New York Academy of Science, 510,* 216–218.

Cernoch, J. M., & Porter, R. H. (1985). Recognition of maternal axillary odors by infants. *Child Development, 56,* 1993–1998.

Colligan, M. J., & Murphy, L. R. (1982). A review of mass psychogenic illness in work settings. In M. J. Colligan, J. W. Pennebaker, & L. R. Murphy (Eds.), *Mass psychogenic illness* (pp. 33–52). Hillsdale, NJ: Erlbaum.

Cometto-Muñiz, J. E., & Cain, W. S. (1984). Temporal integration of pungency. *Chemical Senses, 8,* 315–327.

Corbin, A. (1986). *The foul and the fragrant. Odor and the French social imagination.* (Miriam L. Kochan, Trans., with Roy Parker and Christopher Prendergast). Cambridge, MA: Harvard University Press.

Corbit, T. E., & Engen, T. (1971). Facilitation of olfactory detection. *Perception and Psychophysics, 10,* 433–436.

Costanzo, R. M., & Becker, D. P. (1986). Smell and taste disorders in head injury and neurosurgery. In H. L. Meiselman & R. S. Rivlin (Eds.), *Clinical measurement of taste and smell* (pp. 565–578). New York: Macmillan Publishing.

Craik, F.I.M., & Lockhart, R. S. (1972). Levels of processing: A framework for memory research. *Journal of Verbal Learning and Verbal Behavior, 11,* 671–684.

Desor, J. A., & Beauchamp, G. K. (1974). The human capacity to transmit olfactory information. *Perception and Psychophysics, 16,* 551–556.

De Vries, H., & Stuiver, M. (1961). The absolute sensitivity of the human sense of smell. In W. A. Rosenblith (Ed.), *Sensory Communication* (pp. 159–167). New York: Wiley.

de Wijk, R. A. (1989). *Temporal factors in human olfactory perception.* Doctoral dissertation, University of Utrecht.

Dodd, G. H. (1988). The molecular dimension in perfumes. In S. Van Toller & G. H. Dodd (Eds.), *Perfumery. The psychology and biology of fragrance* (pp. 19–46). London/New York: Chapman and Hall.

Doty, R. L. (1981). Olfactory communication in humans. *Chemical Senses, 6,* 351–376.

————. (1983). *The smell identification test administration manual.* Philadelphia: Sensonics, Inc.

————. (1986). Gender and endocrine-related influences on human olfactory perception. In H. L. Meiselman & R. S. Rivlin (Eds.), *Clinical measurement of taste and smell* (pp. 377–413). New York: Macmillan Publishing.

Doty, R. L., Ford, M., Prety, G., & Huggins, G. R. (1975). Changes in the intensity and pleasantness of human vaginal odors during the menstrual cycle. *Science, 190,* 1316–1318.

Douek, E. (1974). *The sense of smell and its abnormalities.* Edinburgh: Churchill Livingstone.

Duncan, R. B., & Briggs, M. (1962). Treatment of uncomplicated anosmia by vitamin A. *Archives of otolaryngology, 75,* 36–44.

Ebling, F. J. (1977). Hormonal control of mammalian skin glands. In D. Müller-Schwarze & M. M. Mozell (Eds.), *Chemical Signals in Vertebrates* (pp. 17–34). New York: Plenum Press.

Eichenbaum, H. and Cohen, N. S. (1987). Representation in the hippocampus: What do hippocampalneurons code? *Trends in Neurosciences, 11,* 244–248.

Ekman, G., Berglund, B., Berglund, B., & Lindvall, T. (1967). Perceived intensity of odor as a function of time of adaptation. *Scandinavian Journal of Psychology, 8,* 177–186.

Engen, T. (1964). Psychophysical scaling of odor intensity and quality. *Annals of the New York Academy of Sciences, 116,* 504–516.

————. (1972). The effect of expectation on judgments of odor. *Acta Psychologica, 36,* 450–458.

————. (1977). Taste and smell. In J. E. Birren & K. W. Schaie (Eds.) *Handbook of the psychology of aging* (pp. 554–561). New York: Van Nostrand.

————. (1982). *Perception of odors.* New York: Academic Press.

————. (1986a). Children's sense of smell. In H. L. Meiselman & R. S. Rivlin (Eds.), *Clinical measurement of taste and smell* (pp. 316–325). New York: Macmillan Publishing.

————. (1986b). Perception of odor and irritation. *Environment International, 12,* 177–187.

————. (1986c). The combined effect of carbon monoxide and alcohol on odor sensitivity. *Environment International, 12,* 207–210.

————. (1987, September-October). Remembering odors and their names. *American Scientist,* pp. 497–503.

————. (1988). The acquisition of odour hedonics. In S. Van Toller

& G. H. Dodd (Eds.), *Perfumery. The psychology and biology of fragrance* (pp. 79–90). London/New York: Chapman and Hall.

———. (1989). Unpublished data.

Engen, T., Gilmore, M. M., & Mair, R. G. Odor memory (1991). In T. Getchell, R. L. Doty, L. M. Bartoshuk, & J. B. Snow (Eds.), *Smell and taste in health and disease* (Ch. 16, pp. 315–328). New York: Raven Press.

Engen, T., Kuisma, J. E., & Eimas, P. D. (1973). Short-term memory of odors. *Journal of Experimental Psychology, 99,* 222–225.

Engen, T., Levy, N., & Schlosberg, H. (1958). The dimensional analysis of a new series of facial expressions. *Journal of Experimental Psychology, 55,* 454–458.

Engen, T., & Lipsitt, L. P. (1965). Decrement and recovery of responses to olfactory stimuli in the human neonate. *Journal of Comparative and Physiological Psychology, 59,* 312–316.

Engen, T., Lipsitt, L. P., & Kaye, H. (1963). Olfactory responses and adaptation in the human neonate. *Journal of Comparative and Physiological Psychology, 56,* 73–77.

Engen, T., & McBurney, D. H. (1964). Magnitude and category scales of the pleasantness of odors. *Journal of Experimental Psychology, 68,* 435–440.

Engen, T., & Pfaffmann, C. (1959). Absolute judgments of odor intensity. *Journal of Experimental Psychology, 58,* 23–26.

———. (1960). Absolute judgments of odor quality. *Journal of Experimental Psychology, 59,* 214–219.

Engen, T., & Ross, B. M. (1973). Long-term memory of odors with and without verbal descriptions. *Journal of Experimental Psychology, 100,* 221–227.

Estrem, S. A., & Renner, G. (1987). Disorders of smell and taste. *Neurological Disorders in Otolaryngology, 20,* 133–147.

Etgen, G., Wyatt, J., & Carskadon, M. A. (1989). Human olfactory sensitivity in sleep: Preliminary results. Personal communication.

Fanger, P. O. (1988). Introduction of the olf and the decibel units to quantify air pollution perceived by humans indoors and outdoors. *Energy and Building, 12,* 1–6.

Filsinger, E. E., Braun, J. J., Monte, W. C., & Linder, D. E. (1984). Human (homo sapiens) responses to the pig (sus scrofa) sex pheromone 5 Alpha-androst-16-en-3-one. *Journal of Comparative Psychology, 98,* 219–222.

Filsinger, E. E., & Fabes, R. A. (1985). Odor communication, pheromones, and human families. *Journal of Marriage and the Family, 47,* 349–359.

Foreyt, J. P., & Kennedy, W. A. (1971). Treatment of overweight by aversion therapy. *Behavior Research and Therapy, 9,* 29–34.

Gabassi, P. G., & Zanuttini, L. (1983). Riconoscimento di stimoli olfattivi nella memoria a breve termine. *Giornale Italiano di Psicologia, 10,* 51–60.

Garner, W. R., & Hake, H. S. (1951). The amount of information in absolute judgments. *Psychological Review, 58,* 446–459.

Gerbrandt, L. K. (1987). Hippocampal memory deficits. In G. Adelman (Ed.), *Encyclopedia of neuroscience,* Vol. 1 (pp. 488–491). Boston: Birkhäuser.

Gesteland, R. C. (1986). Speculations on receptors cells as analyzers and filters. *Experientia, 42,* 287–291.

Goldstein, H. I., & Cagan, R. H. (1981). The major histocomparability complex and olfactory receptors. In R. H. Cagan & M. R. Kare (Eds.), *Biochemistry of taste and olfaction* (pp. 93–105). New York: Academic Press.

Goodspeed, R. B., Catalanotto, F. A., Gent, J. F., Cain, W. S., Bartoshuk, L. M., Leonard, G., & Donaldson, J. O. (1986). Clinical characteristics of patients with taste and smell disorders. In H. L. Meiselman & R. S. Rivlin (Eds.), *Clinical measurement and taste and smell* (pp. 451–466). New York: Macmillan Publishing.

Gower, D. B., Nixon, A., & Mallet, A. I. (1988). The significance of steroids in axillary odour. In S. Van Toller & G. H. Dodd (Eds.), *Perfumery. The psychology and biology of fragrance* (pp. 47–76). London/New York: Chapman and Hall.

Graziadei, P.P.C., & Monti Graziadei, G. A. (1978). Continuous nerve cell renewal in the olfactory system. In E. M. Jacobson (Ed.), *Handbook of sensory physiology: Vol. 9. Development* (pp. 55–82). Berlin: Springer Verlag.

Green, D. M., & Swets, J. A. (1974). *Signal detection theory and psychophysics.* New York: Krieger.

Gustavson, A. R., Dawson, M. E., and Bonett, D. G. (1987). Androsternol, a putative human pheromone, affects human (homo sapiens) male choice performance. *Journal of Comparative Psychology*, 101, 210–212.

Gustavson, C. R., Kelly, D. J., Sweeney, M., & Garcia, J. (1976). Prey-lithium aversions: I. Coyotes and wolves. *Behavioral Biology, 17*, 61–72.

Halliday, M.A.K., & Hasan, R. (1976). *Cohesion in English*. London: Longman.

Hebb, D. O. (1958). *A textbook of psychology*. Philadelphia and London: W. B. Saunders Company.

Hofstadter, D. (1987, June 1). Profiles (Avigdor Arikha). *The New Yorker*, p. 55.

Horak, J. (1979, September 12). Gas lines need deodorant, not fix, jittery callers told. *Lafayette Journal and Courier*, p. 60.

Hvastja, di L., & Zanuttini, L. (1987). Riconoscimento di odori "noti": Etichette verbali ed indizi contestuali [The recognition of "well known" odors: Verbal labels and contextual cues]. *Richerche di Psicologia, 2*, 46–55.

Jafek, B. W., Moran, D. T., Eller, P. M., Roweley, J. C., & Jafek, T. B. (1987). Steroid-dependent anosmia. *Archives of Otolaryngology. Head and Neck Surgery, 113*, 547–549.

Jellinek, P. (1954). *The practice of modern perfumery* (Translated and revised by A. J. Krajkeman). New York: Interscience Publishers.

Johansson, I. (1990). Flyktiga organiska ämnen i inomhusluft av betydelse för hälsa och komfort [volatile organic compounds in indoor air of significance for health and comfort] (IMM-Report 6/90). Stockholm, Sweden: Karolinska Institut.

Jones, F. N., & Jones, M. H. (1953). Modern theories of olfaction: A critical review. *Journal of Psychology, 36*, 207–241.

Jung, T.T.K., Juhn, S. K., Wang, D., & Stewart, R. (1987). Prostaglandins, leukotrienes and other arachidonic acid metabolites in nasal polyps and nasal mucosa. *Laryngoscope, 97*, 184–189.

Kern, S. (1974, Spring). Olfactory ontology and scented harmonies: On the history of smell. *Journal of Popular Culture*, pp. 814–824.

Keverne, E. B. (1987) Pheromones. In G. Adelman (Ed.) *Encyclopedia of Neuroscience*, Vol. 2 (pp. 944–946). Boston: Birkhäuser.

King, H. E. (1972). Sensory retaining and the problem of human memory. In M. Hammer, K. Salzinger, & S. Sutton (Eds.), *Psychopathology* (pp. 243–259). New York: Wiley.

King, J. R. (1988). Anxiety reduction using fragrances. In S. Van Toller & G. H. Dodd (Eds.), *Perfumery. The psychology and biology of fragrance* (pp. 147–165). London/New York: Chapman and Hall.

Kirk-Smith, M., & Booth, D. (1980). Effect of adrostenone on choice of location in other's presence. In H. van der Starre (Ed.), *Olfaction and taste* (Vol. 7) (pp. 397–400). London: IRL Press.

Koelega, H. S., & Köster, E. P. (1974). Some experiments on sex differences in odor perception. *Annals of the New York Academy of Sciences, 237*, 234–246.

Laing, D. G. (1983). Natural sniffing gives optimum odour perception for humans. *Perception, 12*, 99–117.

Laing, D. G., & MacKay-Sim, A. (1975). Olfactory adaptation in the rat. In D. A. Denton & J. P. Coghlan (Eds.), *Olfaction and taste* (Vol. 5) (pp. 291–295). New York: Academic Press.

Lawless, H. T., & Engen, T. (1977). Associations to odors: Interference, memories and verbal labeling. *Journal of Experimental Psychology, 3*, 52–59.

Lazarus, R. (1966). *Psychological stress and the coping process.* New York: McGraw-Hill.

LeMagnen, J. (1952). Les phénomènes olfacto-sexuels chez l'homme. *Archives of Science and Physics, 6*, 125–160.

Le Norcy, S. (1988). Selling perfume: A technique or an art? In S. Van Toller & G. H. Dodd (Eds.), *Perfumery. The psychology and biology of fragrance* (pp. 217–226). London/New York: Chapman and Hall.

Lipsitt, L. P., Engen, T., & Kaye, H. (1963). Developmental changes in the olfactory threshold of the neonate. *Child Development, 34* 371–376.

Logue, A. W., Ophir, I., & Strauss, K. E. (1981). The acquisition of taste aversions in humans. *Behavior Research and Therapy, 19*, 319–333.

MacFarlane, A. (1975). Olfaction in the development of social preferences in the human neonate. In R. Porter & M. O'Connor (Eds.), *The human neonate in parent-infant interaction.* Ciba Foundation Symposium, Elsevier, Amsterdam, *33*, 103–117.

Mair, R. G., Bouffard, J. A., Engen, T., & Morton, T. H. (1978). Olfactory sensitivity during the menstrual cycle. *Sensory Processes, 2*, 90–98.

McClintock, M. K. (1971). Menstrual synchrony and suppression. *Nature, 229*, 224–225.

Meredith, M. (1987). Trigeminal response to odor. In G. Adelman (Ed.), *Encyclopedia of neuroscience* (Vol. 2) (pp. 1234–1235). Boston: Birkhäuser.

Miller, G. A. (1956). The magic number seven, plus or minus two: Some limitations on our capacity for processing information. *Psychological Review, 63*, 81–97.

Moran, D. T, Jafek, B. W., Carger, R., III, Roweley, J. C., & Eller, P. M. (1985). Electron microsopy of olfactory epithelia in two patients with anosmia. *Archives of Otolaryngology, 111*, 122–126.

Moskowitz, H. R., Dravnieks, A., Cain, W. S., & Turk, A. (1974). Standardized procedure for expressing odor intensity. *Chemical Senses and Flavor, 1*, 235–237.

Mozell, M. M. (1987). Olfaction. In G. Adelman (Ed.), *Encyclopedia of neuroscience* (pp. 874–877). Boston: Birkhäuser.

Mozell, M. M., & Jagodowicz, M. (1973). Chromatographic separation of odorants by the nose: Retention times measured across *in vivo* olfactory mucosa. *Science, 181*, 1247–1249.

Mozell, M. M., Schwarts, D. N., Leopold, D. A., Hornung, D. E., & Scheehe, P. R. (1986). Reversal of hyposmia in laryngectomized patients. *Chemical Senses, 11*, 397–410.

Müller-Schwarze, D. (1977). Complex mammalian behavior and pheromone bioassay in the field. In D. Müller-Schwarze & M. M. Mozell (Eds.), *Chemical signals in vertebrates* (pp. 413–433). New York: Plenum Press.

Murphy, C. (1986). Taste and smell in the elderly. In H. L. Meiselman & R. S. Rivlin (Eds.), *Clinical measurement of taste and smell* (pp. 343–371). New York: Macmillan.

Murphy, C., & Cain, W. S. (1980). Taste and olfaction: Independence vs. interaction. *Physiology & Behavior, 24*, 601–605.

Murphy, C., Cain, W. S., & Bartoshuk, L. M. (1977). Mutual action of taste and olfaction. *Sensory Processes, 1*, 204–211.

Mygind, N., & Lowenstein, H. (1982). Allergy and other environmental factors. In D. F. Proctor & I. Andersen (Eds.), *The nose: Upper airway physiology and the atmospheric environment* (pp. 377–397). Amsterdam: Elsevier Biomedical Press.

Mykytowycz, R. (1977). Olfaction in relation to reproduction in domestic animals. In D. Müller-Schwarze & M. M. Mozell (Eds.), *Chemical signals in vertebrates* (pp. 207–224). New York: Plenum Press.

Nabokov, V. M. (1970). *Mary* (Michael Glenny, Trans.). New York: McGraw-Hill.

Ottoson, D. (1980). Inverkan av organisk lösninsmedel på nersystemet: Functionalla och structurélla studier med lucksystemet som modellorgan [Effect of organic solvents on the nervous system: Functional and electromicroscopic observations with the olfactory system as the model]. Unpublished Report, Arbetarskyddsstyrelsens Bibliotek, Dnr. 77/90. Stockholm, Sweden.

Pedersen, P. E., & Blass, E. M. (1982). Prenatal and postnatal determinants of the first sucking response in albino rats. *Developmental Psychobiology, 15*, 349–355.

Peterson, L. R., & Peterson, M. J. (1959). Short-term retention of individual verbal items. *Journal of Experimental Psychology, 58*, 193–198.

Porter, R., Cernoch, J. M., & McLaughlin, F. J. (1983). Maternal recognition of neonates through olfactory cues. *Physiology and Behavior, 30*, 151–154.

Price, J. L. (1987). Amygdaloid complex. In G. Adelman (Ed.), *Encyclopedia of neuroscience* (Vol. 1) (pp. 40–42). Boston: Birkhäuser.

Proctor, D. F. (1983). The upper airways: Interface between the lungs and the ambient air. *New England Society of Allergy Proceedings, 3*, 378–382.

Proust, M. (1928). *Swann's way* (C. K. Scott Moncrieff, Trans.). New York: Modern Library.

Providence Sunday Journal. Florida city is hit by a severe case of nose pollution (nd.)

Raab, K. H. (1987). Risk assessment of odor counteraction. In B. Seifert et al. (Eds.), *Proceedings of the 4th international conference on indoor air quality and climate* (pp. 700–704).

Rabin, M. D., & Cain, W. S. (1984). Odor recognition: Familiarity, identifiability, and encoding consistency. *Journal of Experimental Psychology: Learning Memory and Cognition, 10*, 316–325.

Rotton, J., Barry, T., Frey, J., & Soler, E. (1978). Air pollution and interpersonal attraction. *Journal of Applied Social Psychology, 8*, 57–71.

Rovesti, P., & Colombo, E. (1973). Aromatherapy and aerosols. *Soap, Perfumery and Cosmetics, 47*, 475–477.

Rozin, P., & Schiller, D. (1980). The nature and acquisition of a preference for chili pepper in humans. *Motivation and Emotion, 4*, 77–101.

Russell, M. J., Switz, G. M., & Thompson, K. (1980). Olfactory influences on the human menstrual cycle. *Pharmacology, Biochemistry, and Behavior, 13*, 737–738.

Salk, J. (1987). Poliomyelitis. In G. Adelman (Ed.), *Encyclopedia of neuroscience* (Vol. 2) (pp. 956–957). Boston: Birkhäuser.

Sarnat, H. B. (1975). Olfactory reflexes in the newborn infant. *Journal of Pediatrics, 92*, 624–626.

Schaal, B. (1988a). Olfaction in infants and children: Developmental and functional perspectives. *Chemical Senses, 13*, 145–190.

————. (1988b). Discontinuité natale et continuité chimio-sensorielle: Modèles animaux et hypothèses pour l'homme. *Annales Biologiques, 27*, 1–41.

Schemper, T., Voss, S., & Cain, W. S. (1981). Odor identification in young and elderly persons: Sensory and cognitive limitations. *Journal of Gerontology, 36*, 446–452.

Schiffman, S. S. (1979). Changes in taste and smell with age: Psychophysical aspects. In J. M. Ordy and K. Brizzee (Eds.), *Sensory systems and communication in the elderly: (Vol. 10). Aging* (pp. 227–246). New York: Raven Press.

Schiffman, S. S., Reynolds, M. L., & Young, F. W. (1981). *Introduction to multidimensional scaling.* New York: Academic Press.

Schleidt, M., & Genzel, C. (1990). The significance of mother's perfume for infants in the first weeks of their life. *Ethology and Sociobiology, 11*, 145–154.

Schleidt, M., & Hold, B. (1982). Human odour and identity. In W. Breipohl (Ed.), *Olfaction and endocrine regulation* (pp. 181–194). London: IRL Press.

Schleidt, M., Neumann, P., & Morishita, H. (1988). Pleasure and disgust: Memories and associations of pleasant and unpleasant odours in Germany and Japan. *Chemical Senses, 13*, 279–293.

Science News. (1989). *136*, p. 374.

Shepherd, G. (1988). Personal communication.

Sherry, D. F., & Schacter, D. L. (1987). The evolution of multiple memory systems. *Psychological Review, 94*, 439–454.

Sommerville, B., & Gee, D. (1987). Research on body odours: New prospects for combatting crime? *International Criminal Police Review*, July-August, English ed., pp. 18–22.

Stoddart, D. M. (1988). Human odor culture: A zoological perspective. In S. Van Toller & G. H. Dodd (Eds.), *Perfumery. The psychology and biology of fragrance* (pp. 3–17). London/New York: Chapman and Hall.

Suskind, P. (1986). *Perfume.* New York: Alfred A. Knopf.

Swanson, L. W. (1987). Limbic system. In G. Adelman (Ed.), *Encyclopedia of Neuroscience* (Vol. 1) (pp. 589-591). Boston/Basel/Stuttgart: Birkhäuser.

Talamo, B. R., Rudel, R. A., Kosik, K. S., Leet, V. M., Neff, S., Adelman, L., & Kauer, J. S. (1989). Pathological changes in olfactory neurons in patients with Alzheimer's disease. *Nature, 337*, 736–739.

Teghtsoonian, R., Teghtsoonian, M., Berglund, B., & Berglund, U. (1978). Invariance of odor strength with sniff vigor: An olfactory analogue to size constance. *Journal of Experimental Psychology: Human Perception and Performance, 4*, 144–152.

Third Karolinska Institute Symposium on Environmental Health. (1970). Methods for measuring and evaluating odorous air pollutants at the source and in the ambient air. *Nordisk Hygienisk Tidskrift, 51*(2).

Thomas, L. (1974). *The lives of a cell.* New York: Viking.

Tisserand, R. (1988). Essential oils as psychotherapeutic agents. In S. Van Toller & T. H. Dodd (Eds.), *Perfumery. The psychology and biology of fragrance* (pp. 167–181). London/New York: Chapman and Hall.

Torii, S., Fukuda, H., Kanemoto, H., Miyanchi, R., Hamauzu, Y., & Kawasaki, M. (1988). Contingent negative variation (CNV) and the psychological effects of odour. In S. Van Toller & G. H. Dodd (Eds.), *Perfumery. The psychology and biology of fragrance* (pp. 107–120). London/New York: Chapman and Hall.

Triedman, K. E. (1981). *On the existence and importance of human pheromones: Social interaction effects on the human menstrual cycle*. Unpublished honors thesis, Department of Psychology, Brown University.

Underwood, B. J. (1957). Interference and forgetting. *Psychological Review, 64*, 49–60.

Van Toller, S. (1988). Emotion and the brain. In S. Van Toller & G. H. Dodd (Eds.), *Perfumery. The psychology and biology of fragrance* (pp. 121–146). London/New York: Chapman and Hall.

Van Toller, S., & Dodd, G. H. (1987). Presbyomsia and olfactory compensation for the elderly. *British Journal of Clinical Practice, 41*, 725–728.

———. (1988). *Perfumery. The psychology and biology of fragrance.* London: Chapman and Hall.

Van Toller, S., Dodd, G. H., & Billing, A. (1985). *Aging and the sense of smell.* Springfield, IL: Charles C. Thomas.

Wang, S. J. (1982). *Scanning of olfactory information in short-term memory.* Unpublished master of science thesis, Brown University.

Whisman, M. L., Goetzinger, J. W., Cotton, F. O., & Brinkman, D. W. (1978). Odorant evaluation: A study of ethanethiol and tetrahydrothipene as warning agents in propane. *Environmental Science & Technology. American Chemical Society, 12*, 1285–1288.

Wingfield, A., & Brynes, D. (1981). *The psychology of human memory.* New York: Academic Press.

Wolpin, M., & Weinstein, C. (1983). Visual imagery and olfactory stimulation. *Journal of Mental Imagery, 7*, 63–74.

Woodworth, R. S., & Schlosberg, H. (1954). *Experimental Psychology.* New York: Henry Holt and Company.

Wysocki, C. J. (1979). Neurobehavioral evidence for the involvement of the vomeronasal system in mammalian reproduction. *Neuroscience and Biobehavioral Reviews, 3*, 301–341.

Yaglou, C. P., Riley, E. C., & Coggins, D. I. (1936). Ventilation requirements. *ASHRAE Transactions, 42*, 133–162.

Index

Garcia, J., 83
Garner, W. R., 78
gas detector. *See* sensor
gas odor, 11
Gee, D., 66
gender difference, 97, 99
genetics. *See* heredity
Genzel, C., 63, 75
Gerbrandt, L. K., 111
Gesteland, R. C., 110
Gilmore, M. M., 104
Goetzinger, J. W., 49
Goldstein, H. I., 66
Goodspeed, R. B., 90
Gower, D. B., 73
Graziadei, C. A., 110
Graziadei, P. P., 110
Green, D. M., 114
Greene, T. E., 42
Gustavson, A. R., 72
Gustavson, C. R., 83

habituation, 18, 25, 116
Hake, H. S., 78
Halliday, M.A.R., 86
hallucination, 4
Hamazu, Y., 22
Hasan, R., 86
hearing. *See* modality comparisons
Hebb, D. O., 93
heredity, 92, 103
hippocampus, 6, 9, 87, 104, 111
histocompatability complex, 66
hits. *See* false alarms
Hofstadter, D., 81
Hold, B., 64
Horak, J., 11
hormones, 98, 103

Huggins, G. R., 40
Hvastja, di L., 85
hypersensitivity, 28, 101
hyposmia, 90, 91, 96
hypothalamus, 101

identification of odor, 10, 78, 84, 115. *See also* odor, naming
illusion, 118
immune system, 67
impression management, with perfume, 60
imprinting pheromone, 66
incidental learning, 6. *See also* odor, learning
individual differences, 15, 41, 52, 63, 89, 97, 100
indoor air, 47
intensity of odors, 36
interference, 32, 40; proactive, 31, 118; retroactive, 82
introspection, 25
irritation, 94

Jafek, B. W., 104, 105
Jafek, T. B., 105
Jagodowicz, M., 69
Jellinek, P., 2, 70, 73
Johansson, I., 43
Juhn, S. K., 103
Jung, T.T.K., 103

Kallmann's syndrome, 73, 104
Kaye, H., 99, 111
Kelley, D. J., 83
Kennedy, W. A., 43
Keverne, E. B., 65
King, H. E., 39
King, J. R., 58

ABOUT THE AUTHOR

TRYGG ENGEN is a professor at Brown University. He is an eminent authority in sensory perception—most particularly in the area of odor perception. He has received much international recognition, including an honorary doctorate from the University of Stockholm, where he also conducts research and teaches.